CONTENTS

UNDERSTANDING ETHNOGRAPHIC TEXTS

PAUL ATKINSON
University of Wales, Cardiff

Qualitative Research Methods
Volume 25

SAGE PUBLICATIONS
International Educational and Professional Publisher
Newbury Park   London   New Delhi

For information address:

 SAGE Publications, Inc.
2455 Teller Road
Newbury Park, California 91320

SAGE Publications Ltd.
6 Bonhill Street
London EC2A 4PU
United Kingdom

SAGE Publications India Pvt. Ltd.
M-32 Market
Greater Kailash I
New Delhi 110 048 India

Printed in the United States of America

Library of Congress Cataloging-in-Publication Data

Atkinson, Paul.
    Understanding ethnographic texts/Paul Atkinson.
        p.   cm. — (Qualitative research methods; v. 25)
    Includes bibliographical references.
    ISBN 0-8039-3936-1 (cloth).   —ISBN 0-8039-3937-X (pbk.)
    1. Ethnology—Authorship.   2. Ethnology—Methodology.   I. Title.
II. Series.
GN307.7.A87   1992
305.8'001—dc20   92-8060
                                                                      CIP

        94   10   9   8   7   6   5   4   3

Sage Production Editor: Judith L. Hunter

EDITORS' INTRODUCTION

The number of ways in which fieldwork-based study can be put forth in words is multiplying rapidly these days. Straightforward versions of plain-speaking ethnographic realism compete with distinct but different forms of *Nouveau Ethnography,* including confession-like first-person accounts, dialogic two-person encounters, culture critique of a prissy high-brow or fashionable low-brow sort, travel logs from far-distant lands or neighborhood bars, formal and ambitious analytic readings of painstakingly detailed local mundane action, and so forth. Some of this reflects the fact that ethnographers are practicing their trade in new locales. But what is odd about the current mix of presentation styles is that regardless of where the work is conducted—among the sheltering palms or deep in the Paris sewers—the texts of a traditional or nouveau bent still rest their slender or fat truth claims on the old ethnographic chestnut that having "been there" provides warrant to hold forth on what one makes of it.

Paul Atkinson worries about how this warrant is carried out in the 25th volume of the Sage Series on Qualitative Research Methods. His intention is not to provide a craft manual for the construction of sturdy ethnography but to order and probe the multitude of ways ethnographic work appears and appears to work. His method is to note what literary conventions attach to certain kinds of ethnograhpic presentations. Such conventions produce recognizable styles or genres, each with their own advantages and disadvantages given the kind of reading one wishes to make of them. Cutting across all styles, however, is a paradox: The more readable an account the less faithful it will seem to those who live in or closely attend to the world it describes (and, of course, vice versa).

Ethnographers certainly wish their work to be read but at what cost to faithfulness? But this is not a matter of rational trade-off and choice for it is certain that not all ethnographers can handle the literary conventions associated with either widely read or particularly faithful ethnography in any other than a clumsy way, thus assuring another unread ethnography (which, properly speaking, is no ethnography at all). The biting point driven home in this monograph is that given styles hold special truths and consequences for the writer, the reader, and the written about. Thus, what Paul Atkinson has to teach us here is not how to choose but what such choice implies in a skillfully comparative and morally conscious way.

—John Van Maanen
Peter K. Manning
Marc L. Miller

ACKNOWLEDGEMENTS

The views expressed in this monograph, for what they are worth, have come from years of teaching and discussing ethnographic research methods with students and colleagues at Edinburgh, Stirling, Davis, and Cardiff. Throughout that time I have had the benefit of Sara Delamont's friendship and colleagueship, as well as the example of her unflagging industry. As ever she has commented on drafts of this work, and has been generous with her help and support.

I am grateful to John Van Maanen and Peter Manning for their editorial support in the preparation of this volume, and to Mitch Allen of Sage Publications. The word processing of this volume has been aided by Pauline Donovan, Elizabeth Renton, and Irene Williams.

UNDERSTANDING ETHNOGRAPHIC TEXTS

PAUL ATKINSON
*University of Wales College
of Cardiff*

1. INTRODUCTION

In this short book it is not intended to review and recapitulate all the strategies and processes involved in writing ethnography. The rapidly growing literature on that topic is too large to review in detail here, and others have done so already.[1]

In any case, this book is not just about "writing ethnography." In many ways my theme is equally the *reading* of ethnography: or rather, the processes of reading that inform the production and reception of ethnographic texts. More precisely still, the focus of this work is the complex intersection between reading and writing that generates "the ethnography." The perspectives outlined here derive from and develop those in a previous work (Atkinson, 1990) but do not repeat them. There are, of course, some aspects that are necessarily touched on in both books, and together they reflect what is—I hope—a consistent approach. That earlier work outlined some broad themes in the rhetoric of ethnographic texts. Here are taken up some more specific topics on the reading/writing of ethnography and the textual representation of social phenomena.

1

The particular theme that runs through this work is the tension between the complexity of social life and the modes of representation conventionally open to the writers and readers of ethnographic research. The work of reading and writing the ethnography has been predicated on a collection of "literary" methods. We have conventionally understood the world through textual devices: distinctive genres and styles; characteristic tropes, or figures of speech; conventions of reporting speech and action. Each convention renders the subject-matter more or less "readable." Each device for readability makes for particular representations and versions of the social world. The ethnographer necessarily imposes certain forms on the phenomena in attempting to make them comprehensible for readers (including him/herself). Likewise, the reader implicitly uses "literary" conventions in attempting to "grasp" the subject-matter of the ethnography. It would be wrong, therefore, to concentrate exclusively on either the "reading" or the "writing" of ethnography to the exclusion of the other. Indeed, it is misleading to do so. Some doctrinaire perspectives that proclaim the death of the author, treating reading and reception as the *only* consideration, take an important insight to absurd extremes. Texts always imply both processes: authors are also readers, and readers also write. Ethnographers do not only write: they are also the readers of their own and others' work.

When the ethnographer writes, he or she does so against the background of a reader's experience and competence. The ethnographer draws on the models given by other published ethnographies, as well as other "texts of general knowledge" (fictional and non-fictional). The reader of ethnography likewise reads against a background of general literate expectancies and assumptions. Indeed, what we might understand as the intellectual field of "sociology" or "anthropology" is largely constituted out of the vast number of relevant texts and their "intertextual" associations. We can recognize distinctive traditions, schools, and tendencies within (and across) the disciplines with reference to how they are written and how they are read.

If one recognizes that meaningful social life is produced and reproduced through the use of language, then one must also recognize that language is constitutive of how social life is represented. This has particular force for the ethnographer. There is a direct parallel between the methods of everyday understanding and the methods of ethnographic inquiry. We look, listen, and ask; we develop ideas and try them out; sometimes we join in, and sometimes we hang back and observe. The difference between the inquiry and its subject-matter rests on the attitude adopted by the researcher. For the ethnographer, the procedures of research are the methods of mundane practical understanding, *grown self-conscious* (Hammersley & Atkinson, 1983). In precisely the same way, the ethnographer uses the methods of everyday accounting—narratives, descriptions, metaphors, analogies, and examples—to reconstruct the social worlds that are the subject matter of books, papers, chapters, and so on. Equally, therefore, those methods of reading and writing need to become the object of critical reflection. They too must be brought to consciousness (Atkinson, 1991; Hammersley, 1991).

The recognition that the academic scholar is an author and a reader, and that academic disciplines are genres of text with their own stylistic conventions, may appear to constitute an assault on the "authority" of the scholar. That there may be no difference in principle between the expert and the everyday account some observers find a threat to the academy. The author loses his or her authority; the disciplines lose their credibility; the boundaries become blurred; the foundations shake. For those wedded to an outmoded and rigid view of scholarly and scientific discourse, a self-conscious awareness of their literary activities can be threatening. Others also find in textual analysis a questioning of "the author" and of his or her "authority"; they too find occasion for a radical critique of the academy. But they celebrate this loss of authority. The "death of the author" is endorsed, or at least the demise of claims to unique and privileged understanding. Literary critical theory is used to confront the implicit legitimacy of scholarly texts. Critics question the taken-for-granted capacity of the anthropologist or sociologist to construct "the" culture, to paint a "true" picture, of the social world captured in the traditional monograph. There is a loss of certainty that is engendered by this approach. The self-confidence of the traditional ethnographic text is supplanted by a more open and speculative approach to scholarly writing (cf. Van Maanen, 1988).

The position I adopt in this book will differ from the two extremes just outlined. It will recognize that our methods of reading and writing in ethnography are thoroughly conventional and contrived; it will endorse the view that our social-scientific texts draw on the same conventions as other literary forms, including fictional types; but it will find no reason for anxiety on that score. Many of the cherished parallels and contrasts with "science" are totally misleading. First, the texts of the natural sciences are as rhetorical as any other (e.g., Bazerman, 1988; Myers, 1990). Secondly, the recognition that all human inquiry and reportage are essentially the same is not a recipe for nihilism or a loss of scholarly standards. For instance, critics and skeptics may say to ethnographers that their work is too like that of other writers. "How does your work differ from journalism?" is an oft-heard challenge.

Rather than getting hot under the collar about the implied charge, one might more usefully recognize that the ethnographer and the journalist have things in common, and that good work in both trades is recognized by similar criteria: it is based on thorough research, ethically and conscientiously conducted, with a systematic review of sources and evidence, and conveyed to the reader through coherent written texts. (The worst kinds of ethnography and the worst kinds of journalism share similar negative traits). In precisely the same way there need be no immediate threat from the fact that many of the "literary" characteristics of ethnography are shared with yet other genres, including fiction. There are complex historical relationships between "litera-ture" and "science," including the social and cultural disciplines (Lepenies, 1988). The undeniable affinities between "fictional" and "factual" modes of writing do not imply that the work of academic scholarship is rendered invalid. Equally, that separation does not negate the significance of aesthetic criteria in the reading and writing of scholarly work.

This is emphatically not an introductory textbook on qualitative research methods. There are already plenty of manuals of that sort, and the literature covers many key aspects of the research process. There are, however, topics that are under-represented in them. Many aspects of ethnographic research remain poorly documented. As I have remarked elsewhere (Atkinson, 1990), there is a general rule that the farther through the overall research process one goes, the thinner becomes the methodological and practical advice that is available. Consequently, the process whereby complex and often confusing arrays of "data" are transformed into written accounts is often taken for granted. The inexperienced ethnographer might be forgiven for thinking that any problems encountered in that activity reflected merely his or her personal failings. Equally mysterious are the earliest phases of research. Most text-books on ethnography implicitly begin once the research site and general approach have been identified. The "pre-history" of the research is almost always invisible. But the later stages and the earliest gestation period may be equally matters of reading and writing. In the earliest days reading is perhaps the main activity. Not only are books gutted for their substance (as the fodder for a literature review, perhaps), but also their form and style may be implicitly learned. It is largely from reading ethnographies that one gains a sense of the genre(s), and encounters models for one's own work. One becomes academically socialized through the texts of others, just as one's own academic apprenticeship culminates in textual production. The shape and style of other ethnographies may guide not just one's own subsequent writing, but equally the course of the fieldwork itself. For the conduct of ethnographic research is shaped by the images and expectations that are entertained as to the final written products.

Ethnography is especially dependent on the resources of natural language. The very term captures the sense of it: ethno-graphy, the writing of culture. The production and reproduction of our sociological knowledge is thoroughly dependent on the "literary" conventions and textual devices used to construct and interpret our written products. When we undertake an ethnographic project, then we are inevitably committed to major efforts of *writing* (Richardson, 1990b; Wolcott, 1990) and *reading* (Hammersley, 1991). We try to write descriptions of cultural scenes and settings, accounts of social actions and events, cultures peopled by credible social actors. The successful construction of an ethnographic monograph is a considerable literary achievement (Krieger, 1979, 1983, 1984), and anyone who has tried to bring it off will be able to appreciate just how major and difficult a task it is. (Perhaps those who have failed to do so will have an even keener sense of its vicissitudes!) After all, the social world does not present itself to us in the form of a thesis, monograph, or journal article. The data that we accumulate day by day, week by week, and month by month do not automatically yield an understanding that is organized in terms of themes and chapters. We all have to struggle to turn the dense complexity of everyday life into a linear structure—an argument that starts on page one, and progresses through a logical sequence, and ends on the final page. The transformation of cultural life into 80,000 words (or whatever) and a series of more or less uniform chapters is achieved through the imposition of some major—more or less arbitrary—frameworks and constraints.

Furthermore, the "data" with which we deal are often themselves textual products. For most classic ethnographers, there is a double process of textual production and reproduction. For the materials with which we deal are in no sense "raw" data. They include "fieldnotes"—texts that are constructed in order to produce day-by-day accounts of the social life we have observed and participated in. So before we come to "write up" the ethnographic report, we have already "written up" our observations and reflections concerning "the field." Indeed, "the field" that is reported on the basis of fieldwork is not a pre-given natural entity. It is something we construct, both through the practical transactions and activities of data collection, and through the literary activities of writing fieldnotes, analytic memoranda, and the like. Writing up, then, is not the mechanical collation and reportage of raw data. It is part of a complex layering of textual production. The ethnography is a version of social reality that is inseparably a matter of textual representations. In this book I shall be dealing with the conventional transubstantiation of fieldwork into written books, theses, and papers. There are, of course, other modes of representation that are available: visual representation by means of photography, film, and video are all possible—as is the use of audio-recording. They are not dealt with in any detail here.

The sections of this book present variations on one theme: examination of how strategies of writing and reading shape and inform our understanding of ethnographic work. The discussion begins with a consideration of how the social realities of "the field" are produced and reproduced as textual achievements. The argument rests on the issues of "readability" and representation. It is suggested that the very notion of "the field" as a site for research may be constituted through our sense of ethnographies as texts. In other words, our sense of the social world is shaped by the sense of what can be written about it. The same issue is raised in relation to two kinds of "data" used by ethnographers to construct their sociological or anthropological analyses, and often interwoven with analytic text to provide vivid examples and "actual types" (Edmondson, 1984; Atkinson, 1990). The reading and writing of "fieldnotes" is one set of practices where the textual production of ethnographic work is starkly revealed. What may be generated as "data" is affected by what the ethnographer can treat as "writable" and "readable." The fieldnote occupies the intellectual space where reading, writing, and ethnographic interpretation meet. Equally important is the activity of "transcription." It is important to note that the representation of actors' speech is an important—but neglected—topic for ethnographic commentary and reflection. Here again, the tension between the readability of the written text and the complexity of the original phenomena is clear. The more readable the account, the more it corresponds to the arbitrary conventions of literary form: the more "faithful" the representation (conventional though it must still be), the less comprehensible it must become. The decisions taken by the ethnographer have profound implications not just for how readable the text may be, but also for how the actors it portrays are "read" and understood. Here, as elsewhere, textual conventions do not merely raise technical or methodological issues: they have *moral* consequences.

I then go on to discuss how types of texts are linked by their shared literary conventions, to produce recognizable styles and *genres*. Here too I shall suggest that the reading and writing of an ethnographic text is influenced by the conventions of genre and tradition. If our sense of "the field" is determined by the form of its text, then equally our sense of how "the field" should be, and how it should be represented, is conditioned by generic expectations and assumptions. Here, therefore, I review a number of issues relating to ethnographic genre; how particular kinds of subject-matter, local traditions, and generational differences are related to differences in style.

I conclude with some remarks on a number of authors who have taken seriously the written character of ethnographic knowledge, and consider some of the contemporary proposals for ethnographic writing, and "postmodern" critiques of traditional ethnographic texts. Here it is suggested that authors in this vein provide valuable lessons and insights, but the approaches are not homogeneous. Some authors introduce varieties of "readability" by the self-conscious and contrived use of literary forms; others self-consciously produce less readable, more complex and problematic texts in the attempt to mirror their conception of the social. There is no solution. The chosen forms are all conventional: there is no textual format that pictures the social world as a perfect simulacrum. The contemporary ethnographer must make choices in the full knowledge of his or her textual practices, and the likely receptions on the part of readers.

It will be apparent from this introduction that this book is not a guide to how to write an ethnography; nor is it quite a guide to how to read an ethnography. It is intended to aid critical reflection and debate rather than to serve as a craft manual. It should inform practice, but does not pretend to offer recipes and exemplary models. There are several excellent texts that can provide more practical help (e.g., Richardson, 1990b; Wolcott, 1990), and there are more general texts on how to write: Becker (1986) is an excellent book of practical support and stimulation. In contrast, this monograph is really about *how to think about ethnographic texts*. In other words, the purpose of this book is to raise a number of issues about how we should conceptualize the textual character of ethnographic work: not just "how to read" or "how to write" an ethnography, but how to understand an ethnography as the product of reading and writing. This understanding does not result in simple prescriptions and maxims. In many ways it creates problems rather than solving or avoiding them. My argument is that those problems need to be faced and solutions—or compromises—recognized as part of the ethnographer's scholarly craft.

One cannot really write about such issues without a sense of the audience for a given text. It is, therefore, appropriate to address the audience for this book itself. Needless to say, I hope that absolutely everybody will buy and read it, but that is not very realistic. It is addressed specifically to professional colleagues and advanced students in sociology, anthropology, and cognate disciplines. They cannot escape the realization that their disciplines have taken a "textual turn." In addition to producing their own texts (dissertations, papers, books), they are required to reflect on the texts that constitute their academic, intellectual field. So although this is not a "how to do it" book, all contemporary practitioners of the ethnographic craft need "how to think about it" books. This book should, therefore, be read in conjunction with more practical manuals of advice on how to conduct research, how to read and evaluate research, and how to write up research.

Note

1. For major studies that cover several social disciplines see: Ankersmit, 1983; Atkinson, 1990; Billig, 1987; Boon, 1982; Brown, 1977, 1987; Clifford, 1988; Clifford and Marcus, 1986; Edmondson, 1984; Geertz, 1988; Kellner, 1989; McCloskey, 1985; Nelson, Megill, and McCloskey, 1987; Richardson, 1990b; Shotter and Gergen, 1989; Simons, 1989; Tyler, 1987; Van Maanen, 1988; White, 1973, 1978.

2. THE FIELD AS TEXT

The theme of this monograph is partly captured by a well-known distinction drawn by Roland Barthes (1974) between "readerly" *(lisible)* and "writerly" *(scriptible)* texts. In the readerly type of literature "the passage from signifier to signified is clear, well-worn, established and compulsory" (Hawkes, 1977, p. 114); the writerly type, on the other hand, "presumes nothing, admits no easy passage from signifier to signified" (Hawkes, 1977, p. 114). Within the contemporary ethnographic canon there is, I suggest, a tension between the readerly and the writerly. In the first place the ethnographer encounters a problematic and complex social world that is not closed or bounded. By contrast, he or she represents that world within the confines of a given textual form. The limits of what can be understood about the world are set by the boundaries of what can be written and what can be read. Although the conventions of ethnographic writing may be questioned and changed, the tension between the *lisible* and the *scriptible* remains. Indeed, in some ways it becomes increasingly problematic.

When we write of reading and writing an ethnography, there is a danger of implying that there is a social reality—"a field"—that exists independently of and prior to the work of the ethnographer. That is not so. The "field" is not an entity "out there" that awaits the discovery and exploration of the intrepid explorer. The field is not merely reported in the texts of fieldwork: it is constituted by our writing and reading. I do not mean that there are no social beings or social acts independent of our observations. Clearly there are. Rather, my view is that "the field" of fieldwork is the outcome of a series of transactions. To begin with, the field is produced (not discovered) through the social transactions engaged in by the ethnographer. The boundaries of the field are not "given." They are the outcome of what the ethnographer may encompass in his or her gaze; what he or she may negotiate with hosts and informants; and what the ethnographer omits and overlooks as much as what he or she observes. Secondly, "the field" is constructed by what the ethnographer *writes*. In other words, our sense of "the field" resides in what may be written and what may be read. There is, therefore, a triple constitution of the field. First, it is constructed through the ethnographer's gaze. Secondly, it is reconstituted through his or her ability to construct a text-of-the-field. Thirdly, it is reconstructed and recontextualized through the reader's work of interpretation and contextualization.

The general issue is readily grasped if we think of the textual arrangements of some standard ethnographic genres and their associated social forms. Van Maanen (1988) notes, for instance, how typical ethnographic styles achieve their form by means of well-established and standardized means: "by pigeonholing materials into well-regarded functionalist or social system concepts . . . ; moving through the constituent parts of a single activity, performance, ritual, or role . . . ; or following a group through a day, a week, or an annual cycle" (p. 65). Although subject to variation between authors and schools of thought, the classic monograph of social anthropology constructed "standard" types of society and, therefore, types of "field." The boundaries of the ethnographer's world-within-reach, implicitly dividing the thinkable from the unthinkable and the known from the unknowable, were inscribed in the internal arrangements of the monographs themselves. Indeed, one can go further: that very fundamental and pervasive idea of the ethnographic monograph in anthropology is iconic of a host of disciplinary assumptions. The monograph embodies the imagery of the lone explorer (or couple, in some cases) and "his" or "her" people. "The people" are themselves contained and unified within the confines of the monograph itself: each society and each culture is thus fixed. The diversity of social forms and processes is stabilized into a kind of "uniform edition" of standard or classic volumes. Thus, as Boon (1983) has argued, the textual arrangements of functionalist anthropology encoded the presuppositions into the very fabric of its monographs. The standard contents of each monograph reproduced the microcosm that was the functionalists' model social system. Each separate society was represented through a standard array of themes and institutions.

Indeed, one may construe the monograph as a kind of "sign" itself. In a fashion reminiscent of the semiotic triangle, the monograph conjoins "an author" and "a field" (society, culture, group) within a concrete representation:

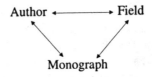

Moreover, just as "the field" is known—that is, it is read—in and through the monograph, so too is the author known through that same process of reading. Not only is there a constant play of intertextuality between the monographs (as with other texts); there is a process whereby "authors" (not necessarily the *persons*) are known and understood in relation to their respective monographs. In other words, for the anthropologist who knows the discipline, it is not just the case that Evans-Pritchard = The Nuer, and Lienhardt = The Dinka, but

Evans-Pritchard : The Nuer :: Lienhardt : The Dinka.

The respective monographs thus provide a textual form of totemic classification and calculus. They become the concrete representations through which human agents and activities become "the field," *and* through which their authors are classified. The Nuer were Evans-Pritchard's: Evans-Pritchard is forever classified by the Nuer. (And, in his case, by the Azande and the Shilluk.) The history of anthropology is the history of monographs. It is a history in which the anthropologist and his or her field are locked in a perpetual embrace. Each constitutes the other in an endless repetition of successive presents. (For the monograph collapses process into pattern, and the here-and-now of the fieldwork experience into the dream-time of the ethnographic present: cf. Fabian, 1983).

Beyond anthropology the monograph also constitutes the field and its author. The urban ethnography defines its own domain. It *names* it—Tally's Corner; The Street Where I Lived; Ship Street; Brown's Lounge—and so implicitly defines its boundaries. Although sociological ethnographers are less likely to be identified with "their" people or locale, they too become linked through the monograph. So Whyte *is* Street Corner Society (1981); Willmott and Young *are* Bethnall Green; Lacey *is* Hightown Grammar (1971). They have other personae too, but we know scholars and their fields through the work of the monograph.

As with the classic anthropological monograph, "the field" is shaped by its textual representations. "Fields" are rendered recognizable and reproducible through the imposition of common textual formats and designs. Each field is unique, and each monograph recognizably different from all others. Yet the particular characteristics of, say, one "community" are discerned against the background of a common genre of "community studies." Each school ethnography implicitly helps to define how each new school might conceivably be described. Each urban gang is characterized in part by previous texts about urban gangs, and so forth. The ethnographer does not encounter his or her field setting without prior implicit models derived in part from the relevant literature; he or she constructs the new ethnography against a background of previous works. Likewise, each reader comprehends the new particulars of each ethnography against a background of prior receptions. The persuasiveness and plausibility, the completeness and cogency of any given ethnography is likely to be judged against the template of prior texts.

It is in that sense, therefore, that one may describe "the field" in textual terms. The ethnographic text is inescapably reflexive, in that it delineates the social phenomena it reports and describes. The argument here is quite different from that proposed by some interpretative anthropologists—most notably Clifford Geertz (1973)—in which social life is approached as if it were a text. That view is not entailed by the proposal that "the field" is textually produced. For it is necessary to recognize that all academic disciplines constitute the objects of their inquiry, and that their respective genres are among the mechanisms used to do so. It is not necessary, however, to believe that all natural and social phenomena are "like" texts. The latter is a fashionable metaphor for social life, and a productive one at that. It stands alongside other grand metaphors of the natural and cultural disciplines, but should not be taken unduly literally. Society is not a kind of text (cf. Brown, 1987). It is, however, true that societies (or segments of society) are academically constructed through their typical representations.

Textual formats make the social world readable. They provide more or less standardized models within which the diversity of social forms can be accommodated. So too do the standard tropes that are used by ethnographers and others to shape their accounts. The textual devices of ethnographic writing portray readable worlds not through the literal but through the figurative uses of language.

The use of tropes (figures of speech) such as metaphor and synecdoche is not a matter of arbitrary or optional embellishment. Its attempted elimination would rob us of the power to describe social events and action in intelligible terms. The removal of metaphorical usage would reduce us to the most banal and meaningless of purely behavioral accounts. Metaphorical usage is fundamental to the analytic force of many social-scientific theories and models. Indeed, as McCloskey (1985), writing specifically on economics, has suggested, the author has but two general strategies: to tell a story or to invoke a metaphor. When the ethnographer wishes to characterize a social world, then he or she can also tell a story or employ metaphorical usage.

The metaphor provides conceptual apparatus and imagery through which we grasp generalities and make comparisons between one setting and another. A successful metaphor can encapsulate a vast array of instances, types, and categories. The analytic metaphor can thus be a sort of crystallisation or condensation of sociological or anthropological understanding. For instance, when one identifies a class or type of "Total Institution" (Goffman, 1961) or "Greedy Institution" (Coser, 1974) as two kinds of setting that incorporate much of the time, effort, and commitment of their members, then those metaphorical designations can convey, allusively, an enormous amount of sociological import. The metaphor invites further comparisons and contrasts. It provides a way of reading not just the original research sites, but a broad range of other sites too. One can employ the metaphor to make comprehensible representations of new settings and occasions. There are direct parallels, for instance, between sociological metaphors, the generic concepts outlined by Lofland and Lofland (1984), and the earlier notion of the sensitizing concept outlined by Blumer (1954). They link and juxtapose. The metaphor may allow one to make the "familiar" seem "strange" and the strange familiar (cf. Delamont, 1981) and so allow the reader and writer to share fresh perspectives on the topic. Equally, well-established metaphors and models can turn the strange into familiar and comprehensible representations.

The metaphorical usage of language thus helps to transform "the field" into the text of the ethnography. It gives shape and consequence to the myriad details of observed life. The trope transforms and illuminates. It brings a given social world into alignment with others in the canon of ethnographic texts. Those texts are also shaped by the reader's and writer's sense of *narrative*. As Richardson (1990a, 1990b) and others have pointed out with increasing force in recent years, the narrative mode is fundamental to the organization of everyday life, and to the organization of the ethnography. The ethnographer draws on and elicits narratives as "data," and reorganizes them into anthropological or sociological narratives in scholarly texts. In that sense, the written ethnography may be thought of as a "metanarrative," or "second-order narrative." The narrative, like the metaphor, furnishes meaning and reason to reported events. Through contextual and sequential presentation, the narrative shapes "the field" into a readable whole.

The narrative presentation of social action reflects the temporal quality of human experience (Adam, 1990). It displays not merely the sequential order of social life, but also its consequentiality. Through narrative the ethnographer—like the historian, the biographer, or the novelist—shapes individual and collective action, character, and motive (cf. Atkinson, 1990). The ethnography embeds and comments on the stories told by informants, investing them with a significance often beyond their mundane production. It includes the ethnographer's own accounts of incidents, "cases," and the like. They too are transformed and enhanced by their recontextualization in the ethnography itself. These narrative instances are collected and juxtaposed in the text so that their meaning (sociological or anthropological significance) is implied by the ethnographer and reconstructed by the reader.

Beyond these fragmentary narratives of persons and circumstances are the metanarratives that shape the ethnography overall. The monograph or paper may be ordered in terms of general narratives. It may take the form of a story of thwarted intentions and unintended consequences, of the display of order in apparent chaos, or of disorder at the heart of rational organization. It can set up a reader's expectations only to deny them. It can transform the reported events of everyday life into the heroic, or endow them with weighty significance. The ethnography can become a morality tale, a high drama, a picaresque tale of low-life characters, a comedy of manners, a rural idyll.

The transformation of "the field" into "the text" is partly achieved, then, via the narrative reconstruction of everyday life. As Richardson (1990a) argues, the narrative mode is a fundamental part of the ethnographer's craft:

If we wish to understand the deepest and most universal of human experiences, if we wish our work to be faithful to the lived experiences of people, if we wish for a union between poetics and science, or if we wish to use our privileges and skills to empower the people we study, then we *should* value the narrative. (pp. 133-134)

Prior to these normative perspectives on narrative is the more elementary observation that narrative (like metaphor) produces a social world that can be written down and read about in recognizable textual formats.

Like all the textual issues considered in this book, the metaphor and the narrative necessarily *transform* social worlds into comprehensible texts. They impose an "as if" quality. They simplify and encapsulate. They characteristically generate "readerly" accounts and narratives, often in the characteristic "realist" mode of conventional ethnography (Van Maanen, 1988). There is, therefore, a potential tension between the "readerly" and the "writerly." The readable narratives and recognizable metaphors necessarily reduce and subsume the complexities and indeterminacies of social life. The standard literary formats of academic monographs (chapters, sub-headings, titles, indexes, etc.) are also arbitrary forms of classification and codification. The comprehensible representation of social worlds is therefore produced via a kind of "symbolic violence" (Bourdieu & Passeron, 1977). Understanding is always bought at the expense of fidelity to the phenomena.

The "realist" account of conventional ethnographic reportage assimilates the social world to taken-for-granted textual forms. There is, indeed, a dialectic between realist literary forms and tacit assumptions about our understanding of the world. In other words, the plausibility and reality-like effect of the ethnographic text relies upon its very artificiality and conventionality (cf. Atkinson, 1990). The ethnographic text has traditionally been a "readerly" text, naturalizing its representations through the implicit use of literary devices (Atkinson, 1982).

In recent years ethnographers have come to recognize the conventional character of "realist tales." They have acknowledged that well-established literary devices reduce the complexity of social life, and impose an unwarranted degree of analytical closure. As the last section of this book discusses, there have been various attempts to provide "alternative" literary forms for ethnographic reportage. "Postmodern" tendencies replace the familiar formats of realist writing with a range of different types. They suggest, perhaps, new limits and new conventions. The overtly literary models are less restricted, and they help to make more problematic the possible relationships between "fields" and "texts." One can no longer take for granted a direct one-to-one relationship between a closed social world and a similarly bounded ethnographic text. The very production and interpretation of "the ethnography" itself becomes more opaque. The character of the semiotic triangle outlined above is also different. The conventional model implied a relatively unproblematic relationship between "author," "text," and "field."

The author of contemporary ethnography stands in a different relationship. Under the older mode, the author was the guarantor of the text's representation of the field. Now he or she indicates the problematic or provisional nature of the representation. I suggested above that Evans Pritchard = The Nuer, in the sense that the relationship between the two and the text that links them was treated as a "transparent" medium. Now, however, Michael Herzfeld (for example) does not stand in the same straightforward relationship to "his" people (Greek peasants). Herzfeld is not "the author of the modern Greeks," but "the author of *writing about* modern Greeks." We should rewrite it as: Herzfeld ≠ Greek peasants. New sets of equivalences emerge. If Herzfeld is the author who makes the anthropology of Greece problematic, then Crapanzano does the same for his Moroccan brotherhoods. There remains, therefore, a discursive domain in which authors, their texts and "their" people stand in relations of equivalence. The value that links them is, however, itself problematic:

$$\text{Herzfeld} \neq \text{Greece} :: \text{Crapanzano} \neq \text{Morocco}$$

Avant-garde ethnographic authors and commentators have therefore sought to replace the readerly text of the field with more writerly possibilities. The relative certainties and comforts of realist, readerly texts of the field are thus replaced with less familiar textual formats. The surface of the text is more faithful to the presumed complexity and fragmentation of the social world. The unifying voice of the ethnographer is subsumed within a "polyvocal" text in which the voices of different social actors are inscribed and read. New literary forms are explored, some of which may violate the cherished models of factual reporting: "fictional" literary modes are deliberately canvassed and adopted. These possibilities create new—as yet underdeveloped—relationships between "fields" and "texts." They still retain the essential and fundamental premise, however: that what can be understood of the social world is both created and constrained by what can be read and what can be written.

Before the ethnography can be realized, however, in whatever form, the "data" of the field themselves depend on textual practices of reading and writing. What can be noted and transcribed is linked to what can be read, and hence to what can be assembled into the ethnographic text. The discussion now turns, therefore, to a consideration of how "fieldnotes" are constituted by textual practices, and will then deal with the transcription of spoken social action.

3. INSCRIPTIONS

The ethnographer constructs and reconstructs social phenomena. The collection and preparation of "data," as well as the various procedures of "analysis," imply the writing and reading of textual materials. There is no datum that exists independently of its inscription in conventional forms; some are visual (film, video, photography), but the great majority of representations are textual. For some forms of representation the literary work is fairly self-evident. For others, the conventional and textual forms are less readily apparent; they are significant for all that. Whatever some practitioners and advocates may think of one or another way of working, none can escape the conventionality of representation. Moreover, the construction of "data" through textual practices is implicative of how the ethnographer makes sense of the research enterprise, how the social world is represented, and how the reader can understand the social world so represented.

In pointing these things out I find no need for undue anxiety or pessimism. There is no great epistemological problem in the fact that neither fieldnotes nor transcripts of permanent recordings are "literal" renderings. Scholarship is not thereby vitiated. The most profound anxieties arise only in relation to the most naive of belief systems. The inescapably textual character of "data" is an offense only if one clings to the view that there might be some other mode of representation. But if it is recognized that there is no possibility of "literal" and unmediated apperception and recording, then many of the most threatening misgivings may be allayed. Mimesis necessarily depends on conventions, not their absence. Consequently, a critical awareness of methodology and epistemology must rest on an understanding of textual methods, but not their denial.

It is obvious that the construction and interpretation of "fieldnotes" is the work of writing and reading. At the most practical of levels, the ethnographer who has employed the "traditional" methods of participant observation will be thoroughly aware of the various tasks involved. The work of the ethnographer expands upon his or her capacity to transform the transactions of fieldwork into a written account. There is need for application and discipline in the daily maintenance of the written record. The novice will be exhorted by textbooks and mentors to "write it down"; to record diligently, lest vital information be lost or only half-remembered; to record fully, concretely. The more experienced, older researcher may find it hard to go on writing detailed notes day after day, week after week. Nevertheless all practicing ethnographers will have some practical experience of the work involved.

Some commentators on method imply that the "conventional" view of fieldnotes treats them as unproblematic sociological or anthropological "data." It is after all a useful rhetorical device in itself to set up the naive ethnographer with a belief in the ability to "capture" social realities through the construction of detailed notes. It is a ploy often used to preface methodological criticisms of ethnographic procedures or to propose superior alternatives. Yet I find it hard to believe that many ethnographers actually cherish the belief that they can mirror "reality" through the diligence and detail of their writing. In reality, fieldnotes reflect acts of what Clifford (1990) refers to as *inscription,* whereby "the flow of action and discourse has been interrupted, *turned* to writing" (p. 51). Clifford goes on:

> Fieldnotes embody cultural facts apparently under the control of their inscriber. . . . But ethnographers can no longer claim this sort of originary or creative role, for they must always reckon with predecessors. . . . The field is more and more littered with "serious" ethnographic texts. One writes among, against, through and in spite of them. This predicament undermines fieldnotes as the privileged empirical basis for a descriptive practice. (p. 55)

Fieldworkers strive to "remember" and to record things as "accurately" as possible. But they are under no illusions as to the purposes and limitations of their work: or if they are, then they have little excuse. The fieldworker should be aware of the fact that there is no complete record to be made, and no neutral medium for its production. The author of fieldnotes (who will also be a reader of them on multiple occasions) should be aware that he or she is just that—an author. The work of observing, participating, listening, and writing is different from that of a stenographer. One is not attempting to transcribe from memory all the many and varied observable and memorable sayings and doings. The notes of the experienced ethnographer will also go beyond an inconsequential listing or jotting of random fragments.

The ethnographer does not just read the fieldnote as an inert and fixed item of information. Ethnographers writing about their own fieldnotes frequently comment on how generally "evocative" their notebooks and typescripts may be, quite beyond just the words on the page. Lederman (1990), for instance, writes of how the note mediates Here and There: "Produced and still smelling of There—musty, smoky, spicy evocations of people and places" (p. 73). The reading and re-reading of notes can thus be a sort of Proustian experience of remembrance. The written notes can never explicitly record all that their author-reader brings to bear on them. It is for this reason (among others) that other ethnographers' fieldnotes are so difficult to analyse and write up without the shared personal experience (Lutkehaus, 1990).

The corpus of fieldnotes make "the field" manageable and memorable. As Lederman (1990) suggests,

> As a corpus, the notes may give us the sense that, for the moment anyhow, they contain the basis for all that can be written about a place: the fundamental intangibility and infinite complexity of social experience reduced to a "thing" which, even when very bulky, has finite dimensions. . . . And their concreteness restores our confidence in the possibility of "grasping" social reality. (p. 89)

Yet, as the same author suggests, the activity of using that corpus of notes shows it to be "not a fixed repository of data from the field but a reinterpretable and contradictory patchwork of perspectives" (Lederman, 1990, p. 90).

The fieldnote is thus a kind of intermediate text, neither "raw" data, nor finished product. It is, as Jackson (1990) suggests, a "liminal" text, and Bond (1990) captures several of its ambivalences:

> Fieldnotes are a product of past interactions and contain a refraction of past occurrences. They are neither fully discourse nor fully texts but possess attributes of both. They unite the culturally and historically specific with the analytically general. They are tied into a local world of knowledge and yet transcend it, providing the preliminary base for synthetic cultural constructions. They are fixed, autonomized, and open, yet they are mutable, dependent, and closed. They are the products of multivocality, the creation of a number of voices. They are the arena of experimentation, translation, and interpretation. They are acts of collaboration, negotiated constructions of aspects of reality whose reality is not always discernible. (p. 286)

Indeed, one could argue that the construction of fieldnotes does not rest so much on what is "memorable" but on what is "tellable." The fieldnote depends very largely on what the author can construct into a coherent narrative or descriptive account. The worked-up notes of the long-term field researcher are not "notes" in the sense that they await "analysis." They do not just depend upon the meaning and significance that analysis bestows retrospectively. They are not the inert accumulation of unconnected sense-data and recordings. They are already encoded with interpretative qualities. Ethnographers do not have to be aware of the full implications and analytic possibilities to have at least some insight into the fact that in writing "notes" they are *constructing* texts and thereby *reconstructing* versions of the social world.

The text of the field already looks forward to "other" texts. As the fieldnote is written, it is projected towards those future acts of writing and their products where its significance will be fulfilled and completed—"the ethnography." The completed monograph or paper will furnish a domain wherein the note's meaning will be found. Hence the fieldnote must look forward to this epiphany. Its revelation will prove another occasion for the "telling" of its message. As the ethnographer accumulates the stock of field data in the notebooks and journals, then, he or she is like the seasoned raconteur who stores up tales that are worth recounting. The stock-in-trade of the ethnographer consists of events and scenes that are describable, and descriptions that may be transmuted into further sociological or anthropological accounts.

Little is known about the production and use of fieldnotes. Their construction and interpretation has been part of the tacit craft knowledge that is handed on from generation to generation as part of the oral culture of various disciplines. The collection of essays by anthropologists on the topic (Sanjek, 1990) is a rare document from that point of view; and even that volume provides only a few, briefly tantalising glimpses of actual fieldnotes themselves. It is, moreover, noticeable that a recurrent theme in those essays is the *privacy* normally afforded these texts. Indeed, for some anthropologists at least, the fieldnote seems to be a "sacred" text, imbued with powerful and dangerous qualities (Jackson, 1990). The sacred texts of field experience seem to contrast with more profane discussions of general anthropological theory and method. It is, perhaps, a reflection of contrasting disciplinary cultures that sociologists, although also treating fieldnotes as personal, seem much less likely than anthropologists to invest their notes with such power. Sociology may just be a more "profane" discipline in general. It is therefore hard to comment empirically on the practices and intentions of ethnographers in general. But limited evidence and personal experience combine to suggest that, if only often at a preconscious level, fieldnotes are constructed with a view to their later readability, and the subsequent tellability of their contents. One does not always have to think consciously "this will make a good vignette" in order to have a general sense of writing "now" with a view to "later" texts.

The fieldnote is, therefore, part of a system of retrospective-prospective relationships with other texts of ethnography. As has just been suggested, it looks forward to that text of culmination, in which the project is fulfilled. It also looks back to other ethnographic texts. For if the "note" is shaped by a sense of what is recountable as ethnographic evidence or example, then it is conceived and executed by virtue of the ethnographer's acquaintance with prior texts of the field, including published accounts (many of which will embed fragments of their antecedent notes as examples). In the absence of any explicit training or methodological precepts on the subject, I know that I modelled my own fieldnote style on the lengthy extracts reproduced in the monographs of admired authors. I was, for instance, particularly impressed by the fieldnote extracts I found in Olesen and Whittaker's ethnographic account of student nurses (1968). They struck me at the time as conveying particular "sensitivity" and "insight." I tried to emulate them when I started making notes in a similar setting, a medical school (Atkinson, 1981). I remember having a semi-conscious desire to include suitably reflective notes, combining a degree of introspection and commentary with well-written descriptive accounts. More generally, one's reading of published work by Chicago-school sociologists and others working in the same style prompted by a particular perspective on the proper making of fieldnotes. It was clear to a novice that fieldnotes ought to be worked-up narrative accounts that were suitable for reproduction as illustrative extracts in published accounts. That sense of "proper" fieldnotes was sustained by reading the few sources where lengthy extracts were available to public scrutiny (e.g., Junker, 1960). In this way, conventions and traditions may be established and transmitted in a tacit manner, and in the absence of any direct personal mentors. The fieldnote does not, therefore, exist in isolation. At the time of its production the fieldnote enjoys relationships of "intertextuality." It is, incidentally, noticeable that sociologists have more commonly included fieldnote extracts as illustrative and supportive "data" in published work than have anthropologists. Geertz (1960) is cited as an unusual case (Clifford 1990).

From my own earliest days as a fieldworker, my "data" were shaped by my own reading of previous texts. Equally, I was aware, and continued to be aware, that I was making my "notes" with a view to their subsequent appearance in published materials. One does not expect *all* one's notes to appear, of course, but in principle one recognizes that they will not remain entirely private documents. I suspect that many fieldworkers have found themselves thinking something like "These notes will make a great example," or "I can use this incident to make a good story one day," or "This will go into my autobiographical confessional in due course." I know that I have sustained myself through the drudgery of fieldnote writing with consolations of that sort.

The ethnographer, then, writes what is "writable," in the light of past writing and with a view to subsequent writing. Although there are few guidelines available in the public domain, there is every reason to believe that fieldworkers develop a sense of appropriate style from their reading of published work and the work of their role models. It is, therefore, highly probable that there are distinctive traditions and genres of fieldnotes that are characteristic of particular schools and disciplines. It would certainly be congruent with the general perspective adopted in this book to propose that rhetoric is inescapably constitutive of "paradigms." The ethnographer will also be aware that fieldnotes are not hard and fast "data" because their meaning and significance are never fixed. The corpus of notes is always open to repeated reading and re-reading. The ethnographer is actively engaged with the texts, not just as their author, but as an interpreter too. The fieldnote is an "open" text through which the ethnographer may derive alternative meanings. (By which I do not mean to imply that there is an entirely arbitrary relationship between the notes and their readings. The recognition that interpretation is an active process is not equivalent to an endorsement of entirely whimsical acts).

Although it is not necessarily the case, the fieldnotes may embody the processes of reading and re-reading. The physical appearance of the text can encode the interpretative processes at work. The notebooks and typescripts or printouts become a kind of palimpsest that records the various moments of interpretation (Farran, 1985). Texts of fieldnotes do not remain inert. The ethnographer annotates his or her notes. There are various practical methods by which that work can be done. Notes may be marked with jotted marginalia and other glosses—equivalent to index terms or other aides-mémoires. Or the glosses may be more formally conceived in terms of "codings." The narrative or the interview transcripts may have keywords attached to them, to be used for sifting, searching, and retrieving segments that relate to a given theme. In recent years, the procedure of coding has been given greater significance as a consequence of various computer software applications for text analyses: they require that segments of the text be marked by the attachment of code words. In a similar way, the use of "hypertext" software provides a contemporary version of glossing and annotation (Tesch, 1990).

Whatever the form of the representations—from marginal jottings to sophisticated computer-generated files—their general character remains the same. There is always a dialectical relationship between "the notes" and the "codings" or the marginalia. Each provides a way of reading the other, and as the analyst reads the materials, so significance is "found" through the interplay of these textual elements. The codes and glossings indicate *how* the segment is to be understood (and there may be multiple readings indexed by multiple codes); the actual segment of "data" gives the concrete meaning of the generic or cryptic annotation. Thus the textual annotations, and their physical layout on the page, provide ways of reading and re-reading. The work of "analysis" and "interpretation" thus involves the ethnographer in a highly active engagement with the texts of the field.

The same is true of other "texts of the field." The construction of memoranda—theoretical, methodological, or empirical—is widely endorsed by advocates of grounded theorizing. The ethnographer accumulates documents that record the reflective dialogue of fieldwork experience. Again, those documents engage with the other texts of "data," "literature review," and so on. The products of reflection are yet further textual materials. What can be thought depends on what can be written. To a considerable extent the process of analytic reflection involves writing about writing. Close inspection of the processes of "grounded theorizing," for instance, reveal them as repeated activities of reading, annotating, writing, and re-reading (Strauss, 1987; Strauss & Corbin, 1990).

Fieldnotes and memos are not the only textual materials that are used as resources in the production of an ethnography. Transcripts of interviews or of naturally occurring interactions are important varieties of data that are used in qualitative research of all sorts. They too depend on textual conventions for their representation.

4. TRANSCRIPTIONS

Textual conventions exert a powerful influence on the representation of informants' or other social actors' own words. The naive might think that there is no problem in the factual reporting of what people say. The author has no need to engage in the kind of invention required of the playwright or novelist. The ethnographer, after all, has no need to contrive plausible dialogue or monologue in order to convey actors' speech. The ethnographic author *has* their speech (noted or recorded). Surely, the task is merely to select and reproduce extracts of the original talk in order to report those data faithfully. Clifford refers to this as *transcription*. It is a broader set of activities than just the technical work of "transcribing" audio-tapes. Transcription also implies writing down "already formulated, fixed discourse or lore" (Clifford, 1990, p. 57). It includes much classical anthropological fieldwork, such as "taking dictation, recording the myth or magical spell" (Clifford, 1990, p. 51), as well as the recording of interviews and other spoken social action. Here is clearly illustrated the problem of "readability." Informants cannot "speak for themselves." In order to give an impression of it we have to select, edit, and *represent* their spoken narratives. Moreover, the more *comprehensible* and readable the reported speech, the less "authentic" it must be. The less the ethnographer intervenes, the more delicately he or she transcribes, the *less* readable becomes the reported speech. Clifford (1990) suggests that in contrast to "inscription," transcription implies a different power relationship between fieldworker and informant: "The authority of the researcher who brings passing, usually oral, experience into permanent writing is decentred" (p. 58). This contrast is misleading, however, for it overlooks the textual work ethnographers bring to bear in making recorded speech readable.

In practice the reporting of informants' talk is as dependent on textual convention as any other element of the text. Any and every method for rendering spoken language is found to be conventional. There is no such thing as a "natural" mechanism for the representation of speech. Orthography, punctuation, type-setting—these are all textual methods through which speech is reconstructed and rendered accessible to the knowledgeable reader. In fact, ethnographers have used a very wide range of styles to represent their data. Each has its effects on the reader. Each may be used—consciously or unconsciously—to convey different interpretative connotations. The different conventions may allow the author to construct informants in quite different ways. The representation of speech, moreover, helps to impart particular qualities and characteristics.

It is often claimed as a strength of ethnographic and other qualitative research that social actors may be allowed to "speak for themselves." And indeed it is a noticeable feature of many ethnographic texts: they are often sprinkled liberally with direct quotations from actors. Sometimes entire texts comprise personal accounts. The cognate genre of the life-history is, of course, especially dependent on the subject's own narratives. In such contexts the accounts and quotations may be thought of as "data." But they are inescapably dependent on textual conventions that are in turn implicative of writers' and readers' interpretations.

Nonetheless, one must be careful not to rely uncritically on the "authenticity" of the modern recording. The verbatim record, for instance, is normally transcribed, and the transcription itself depends on the *conventional* representation of speech. The ethnographer of talk must use textual conventions and representations to convey the data to his or her reader. Just as the representation of talk in fictional writing is dependent on certain textual (including typographical) conventions, so the construction of scholarly transcripts depends on conventional typographical resources. They are themselves matters of interpretation, and *can* be thoroughly implicated in the writer's preoccupations and presuppositions, "readability," "accessibility," and the like. Moreover, the representation of speech can be used to convey the status and character of the speaker. The choice of conventions is thus a choice about the representation of persons as social and moral actors in the text.

Some ethnographers have constructed their accounts almost exclusively through the first-person narratives of their informants. The strategy can be a powerful one. In the hands of a skillful author, the resulting text can have the appearance of a vivid and privileged reconstruction of the speaker's experience. A social world may be conveyed dramatically through the voice of the informant. A variety of narrative accounts can provide a shifting point of view: a kaleidoscope of contrasting or complementary perspectives is provided through a variety of voices.

Oscar Lewis, in his accounts of everyday life in the "culture of poverty" of Mexico City or Puerto Rico, is a classic exponent. He reconstructed the Spanish speech of his informants into extended, highly readable first-person narratives in English. Books like *The Children of Sanchez* (1961) or *La Vida* (1965) are composed out of juxtaposed accounts by family members, each of whom provides a different view of a shared life-world. Lewis's first-person narratives are successful in several ways. The books are among the most widely read works of cultural anthropology. Many readers will have been left with lasting impressions of poverty in the tenement and the slum. The vivid accounts did more to convey Lewis's idea about the culture of poverty than any extended analytic exposition could ever have done. Lewis's overt anthropological interventions in the books are restricted to rather brief introductory essays. The rest is devoted to the lengthy narratives in which the various characters "speak for themselves."

This is not the reality, however. (I do not mean that Lewis practices deception). The characters who speak for themselves in Lewis's texts, do so in voices and in narratives that are highly contrived and reconstructed by Lewis himself. The narratives are edited into coherent, extended texts. No one person—whatever his or her cultural origins—ever spoke such narratives with that assurance and precision. In Lewis's hands what must of necessity have been fragmentary and repetitious become seamlessly smooth. His narrators do not stumble and falter; they do not lose the thread; they do not break off to change the subject or do something more pressing than talk to the ethnographer. They all turn out to be extraordinarily adroit story-tellers. The reader's attention will be held equally by each of the narratives.

In practice, of course, we know that Oscar Lewis took considerable liberties in constructing "their" accounts. The editorial hand has exercised considerable licence, and the role of the anthropologist has been a *creative* one. In one sense, the work of the anthropologist is visible to all attentive readers, quite apart from any explicit statement on his part. We can tell that the books are contrivances. The careful juxtaposition of the accounts is transparently artful. The narratives are clearly reconstructed: they are too lengthy and too "literary" to be the actual transcripts of single tellings. They bear none of the tell-tale signs of spontaneous speech. They are too "smooth": everyday speech is less fluent, less grammatical, and less readable.

Crapanzano (1986) constructs his account in a way very similar to Lewis's method. His book consists very largely of first-person narratives by white South Africans, in what is an undeniably arresting set of accounts from a politically dominant but culturally muted group. The work has been categorized as an example of contemporary "multivocal" ethnography: Crapanzano grants the informants their individual "voices," rather than subsuming them all under his own authorial jurisdiction. In practice Crapanzano does not simply report and juxtapose those voices. He exercises a great deal of tacit and invisible authorial work in collating, editing, and rewriting the personal narratives. The original contexts of their production (such as the interviews and conversations with Crapanzano) are lost to view. Each character is assembled by Crapanzano out of the fragments of narrative available to him, and then freed to address the reader directly, to the accompaniment of occasional asides from Crapanzano. His or her words are fashioned into highly coherent and cogent narratives. Like Lewis before him Crapanzano thus invests his characters with particular kinds of "voices." Each of the Afrikaners, in his or her own way, confronts the reader as an individual hero or heroine in his or her own life-world. This is an *accomplishment* of the authorial activity of the anthropologist. Character is "inscribed," but speech is "transcribed."

Oscar Lewis and Vincent Crapanzano represent one end of a spectrum, and one response to a recurrent dilemma. To what extent should the ethnographer exercise editorial control in order to render the informants' words more coherent and more readable? It is a problem faced by all qualitative researchers who ever wish to quote their informants. If we quote a completely unvarnished version (not that *that* is ever entirely possible), then it may be so difficult to read (because so fragmentary, so far from standard discourse, so full of hesitations and similar phenomena) that the sense of the utterances is all but lost to view. If we adopt the Oscar Lewis solution, then we run the danger of misrepresenting the original speech and rendering it implausibly fluent.

The author who renders the spoken accounts in well-turned prose, elegantly grammatical and without hesitations, is engaged in a task of textual conversion. The *spoken* narrative is translated into the conventions and appearances of *written* discourse. What *reads* like spontaneously natural speech is a highly conventionalized reconstruction or representation. The use of more-or-less standard punctuation or the textual devices of layout (starting each new conversational turn on a fresh line, using punctuation marks) are devices so familiar we remain unaware of them. The average reader will only become aware of the conventions when—as in many modern works—they are not adhered to in the "normal" manner. The ethnographer draws on the same discursive and textual mechanisms in contriving "natural" speech.

The other extreme is to represent the "original" speech in such a way that preserves features of spontaneous speech. In order to do so, of course, the social scientist must again use highly contrived conventional methods. Whereas the first strategy just outlined assimilates the spoken account to the "common" stock of textual representations, the second draws on highly specialized techniques. In recent years the interests of sociologists and anthropologists have converged with those of cognate disciplines to focus on the detailed examination of naturally occurring language. The particular intellectual commitments of conversation analysis, discourse analysis, narrative analysis, folklore (ethnopoetics), and the like differ in their respective emphases. Nevertheless, they share much common ground in the detailed treatment of spoken language.

Despite the considerable detail in which extracts of language are represented in transcriptions, the latter are not, of course, "literal" transcriptions. They are conventional. Moreover, the particular use of the relevant conventions is a matter of interpretation, and may be intended to encourage specific responses and interpretations on the part of the reader. For instance, one of the best known sociolinguists to have directed attention to spoken language is William Labov. Labov's pioneering work on Black English Vernacular is rightly famous not only among linguists, but also among sociologists and educational researchers. His account of the "logic of non-standard English" (1969) is a much-cited and often-anthologised demonstration of how non-standard dialect may be used to express coherently logical thought-processes. The analysis rests heavily on the speech of one respondent, "Larry." In the course of an interview Larry provides a vigorous account of "what happens to you after you die." Labov reads the relevant extract as a taut, idiomatic expression of a series of propositions. He also contrasts Larry's talk with that of a speaker of standard English, proposing that not only are the differences merely stylistic but also the non-standard English conveys *more* information and a more cogent argument.

What is less well known, perhaps, is the perceptive commentary on Labov's work by Cooper (1984). He persuasively argues that Labov himself has allowed his preconceptions and interests to colour the analysis—even to the extent of biassing his punctuation of Larry's speech! It is, of course, obvious on reflection that any punctuation of reported speech is a con-ventionalized imposition on the stream of utterances. It is at best a rough-and-ready representation of patterns of intonation, amplitude, tempo, and pausing. Since the utterances of natural speech rarely correspond to the grammatical constructions of "correct" written language, the use of standard punctuation markers is a matter of interpretation. Cooper suggests that Labov inadvertently prejudges his analysis of standard and non-standard English. He punctuates Larry's speech in a very "sympathetic" manner, so enhancing the apparent cogency of Larry's argument (which he further graces with a translation into more explicit logical propositions). The argument is, then, that we can strongly influence the apparent character of our informants in the eyes of readers by our choice of textual conventions. By choice of punctua-tion a narrative can be made more or less readable, more or less coherent, more or less strange to the reader.

The same sort of argument can be extended from punctuation to spelling. If we do not use strict phonetic transcription (poorly understood by most social scientists), then we are faced with all sorts of decisions about orthog-raphy. To what extent do we use standard orthography to represent variations of accent and style? There is not space to enter into this complex topic here, but a few problems and dilemmas can be noted. First, in the absence of an "etic" transcription, the actual interpretation of the written form depends on (a) the accent of the *reader* and/or (b) the reader's prior knowledge of the reported speaker's accent. Secondly, there are frequently arbitrary bound-aries to be drawn between "standard" and "non-standard" spelling. In every-day speech there are many fine gradations between a clear, unambiguous "I don't know" and "I dunno" (not to mention semantically equivalent utter-ances one might have to represent as something like "A-u-know"). But where does one draw the line? A more or less continuous variation is translated into discrete categories. If one represents a great deal of speech in non-standard spellings, then the reader will likely find it barely intelligible—though it may be comprehensible in its original spoken form. Further, an over-liberal use of non-standard spellings can create a negative typification of the character in the text.

The latter is an obvious danger precisely when we are dealing with ethnic minorities and other non-standard dialect/accent users. We severely distort things if we "transcribe" them apparently speaking with Received Pronunciation. Equally, however, we may on many occasions find it necessary to avoid the embarrassing effect associated with some fictional forms, such as the representation of Southern Black American that creates the "Uncle Remus" image, London working-class speech in Dickens, the representation of "stage Irish," and so on. Apparently when Oscar Hammerstein adapted Bizet's opera *Carmen* to make *Carmen Jones*, set in a U.S. parachute factory rather than a Seville cigarette factory, and among black boxers rather than Spanish toreadors, he introduced a good deal of "stage" black American speech. Carmen ends her seductive *habanera* with "If I love you, dat's de end of you," and the fighter Husky Miller begins his version of the Toreador Song with "Stan' up an' fight until you hear de bell."

A careless representation of "otherness" can readily lead the writer into what Preston (1982, 1985) calls the "Li'l Abner Syndrome." Preston shows how some sociolinguists, folklorists, and others use conventions of orthography to produce the textual equivalents of dialect forms. Common examples are the use of forms such as *sez, wuz, wun*. When Hammerstein rewrote *Carmen*, he included *fewcher* for *future*—quite gratuitously. Preston suggests that such forms "serve mainly to denigrate the speaker so represented by making him or her appear boorish, uneducated, rustic, gangsterish, and so on" (1985, p. 328). He goes so far as to propose that virtually all respellings "share in this defamation of character" (p. 328).

The sustained representation of non-standard forms or regional/class accents is one way in which the "subjects" of the reported speech may be represented as "other" than, different from the reader *and* the ethnographer. Irrespective of the actual individuals, the implied author and reader of most texts share the speech and the written style of the literate intelligentsia. An affinity between the reader and the reported narrator may be implied by the "standardization" of the speech, however. The life-histories and narratives that Oscar Lewis created were not reported in (translated) representations of working-class dialect or accent. The effect is, perhaps, to universalize their reported experiences; they may, too, be invested with greater gravitas and dignity in the eyes of the average reader. Short of unreadable "etic" representations, therefore, the ethnographer who would have his or her informants "speak for themselves" is faced with a number of decisions. Some degree of arbitrary imposition is necessary, and these decisions will have implications for just how those social actors are constructed in the text. The reflective ethnographer will need to be sensitive to the ways in which his or her representation of speech establishes the speaking subjects as "Others" in a dialogue of difference, or assimilates them to a complicity of identity with ethnographer and reader.

5. GENRES

Genre constrains our sense of the readability and the writerly quality of an ethnography. That sense is important insofar as it provides expectations as to what a given social world *should* look like. We know other societies (indeed, much of our own society) through their associated ethnographies, and so they become normative in defining the appropriate forms for understanding societies in general. An ethnography does not just describe a given society or culture; it makes claims that this is an especially appropriate representation. The genre(s) of ethnography give readers and writers exemplary texts against which they can evaluate such claims.

Each monograph, each "ethnography," is unique. It describes and analyses aspects of a particular social setting and social world. However much the author may seek to generalize, to compare, and to theorize on a grand scale, the work is necessarily grounded in the local. The ethnography is bound in time and place. The ethnography is uniquely shaped by the sensibilities and style of its individual author. The ethnographer is, we know, the "research instrument" par excellence. The fieldwork is the product of a personal and biographical experience. Moreover, the text in which that fieldwork is finally (or provisionally) reconstituted is an authored work. Inevitably, it reflects the "literary" style of the individual sociologist or anthropologist.

Equally, each monograph has important similarities and affinities with others. There are various dimensions of "intertextual" relations that construct the intellectual field of the works in question, and which "place" the individual work vis-à-vis others. If one thinks of "the ethnography" as one super-ordinate kind of text, spanning various disciplines, then it also makes sense to think of a range of *genres* of ethnographic writing. Those genres will be constituted by various criteria: there are no hard-and-fast discriminations to be made. Different criteria that may be invoked will partition the field in different ways.

It is, however, necessary to consider issues of "genre" for several reasons. Most importantly, without a sense of similarities, traditions, "schools," and the like, the ethnographic field becomes just an array of undifferentiated texts. If we concentrate solely on the rhetorical characteristics of "ethnography" in general, then there is a consequent loss of precision. For all the commonalities between all ethnographies, there are very clear continuities of tradition, and differences between traditions. Their various types may be read and defined according to various criteria: theoretical orientation; disciplinary allegiance; empirical subject-matter; locale; nationality. In practice, of course, they intersect. One would expect, say, a U.S. cultural-anthropological text of an interpretative turn to differ in its textual formats and devices from a British structural-functionalist monograph.

The mapping of genres and traditions in this field is underdeveloped. There have been some advances within the anthropological discourse; the sociological domain remains all but uncharted. The exploration of anthropological genre has focused on the intersection of subject-matter and orientation, with particular reference to the constitution of *region*. A number of British authors have begun to document the production of regionalism in anthropological texts and traditions. In doing so (and, in a sense, self-referentially) they explicitly distance themselves from U.S. analysts of anthropological texts. The British authors argue that U.S critics have tended to produce a generalized, essentialized view of "anthropology." Likewise, they pronounce a good deal on how anthropological discourse has characterized "the other." In so doing, they overlook the *particular* ways in which "others" have been defined and described; how a particular regional or local tradition is produced and reproduced. *Pace* the "pure" textual critics, the fieldwork experience is not just the confrontation—or the dialogue—between a "Western" observer and an alien "Other." That encounter—or rather a host of fieldwork encounters—is engaged in and interpreted within an intellectual context already framed by a textual tradition: "The regional tradition influences the entry of the "working" ethnographer into a "field" imaginatively charted by others" (Fardon, 1990a, pp. 24-25). There is no implication here that "the field" is determined totally by its textual lineaments, but there is powerful evidence of their influence.

Among the many persuasive and thoroughly documented essays in the Fardon collection on regions (1990b), several show the very particular shaping of regional traditions. Strathern (1990), for instance, shows how Melanesia was defined by a literature of absences, negations, and inversions. James (1990) furnishes a striking comparison of the writing on Sudan and Ethiopia. The two contiguous territories have elicited very different textual traditions. The Sudanese corpus has been central to the development of modern anthropology. The Ethiopian, by contrast, has been marked by an "Orientalist" literature, evocative of exotica and impressionistic in style. This example—like many others in the anthropological canon—also serves to highlight the significance of individual authors in the establishment of regional or other traditions. The Sudanese literature finds Evans-Pritchard as inspiration and model (cf. Geertz, 1983, on Evans-Pritchard's distinctive style). In turn the Oxford department he chaired institutionalised and legitimated his particular style. The enduring representations and versions of "Africa" are also explored (Tonkin, 1990; Werbner, 1990; Parkin, 1990). The regionalization of sub-Saharan Africa is a fascinating history of the interplay of institutional, empirical, theoretical, and rhetorical tendencies. The point is not simply that anthropology has partitioned the world into different arbitrarily defined regions and culture areas. It has also invested them with defining characteristics and marks. Regions, as well as individual "tribes" or "peoples," are thus signified and demarcated by the presence or absence of a restricted range of structural or cultural traits. Equally, of course, the "world" as studied by anthropology is not coterminous with the world in general. It is differentially marked and valued. Some regions are dense with significance, heavily populated with historical and recent monographs. Others are all but uncharted and devoid of significance, or but latterly "filled in." For instance, as Gilsenan (1990) remarks of his entry into anthropological research: "To us students the southern Sudan was central, Egypt peripheral; New Guinea a vital and Lebanon a dead space. The region [Middle East] was indeed not so much peripheral, I suppose, as absent" (pp. 226-227).

It is ironic and revealing that Fardon's collection is in itself constrained by the classificatory schemes the authors confront. That is obvious in the contents, which are arranged in the "standard" divisions and affinities: Hunter/Gatherers; Sub-Saharan Africa and Melanesia; Asia. Equally revealing are the absences from the text: no Northern or Central Europe; no Mediterranean; no sub-Arctic America. The category of Hunter-Gatherers is not matched by, say, peasant or urban populations. None of these British-based authors writes about anything or anybody in Britain. It is, in fact, a celebration as much as a critique of "proper" anthropology and its genres. Critical reflection here maintains boundaries rather than breaking them down. The authors implicitly inscribe that profoundly characteristic exclusiveness of British anthropology. They are slightly patronising of U.S. textual critics, although praising them for their limited insights; they are anxious to distance themselves from such "others" as the "Orientalists"; they drop in autobiographical and biographical details of their own intellectual genealogies; they are as clannish and as "tribal" as the anthropological descriptions that they question.

Mediterranean ethnography has in fact given rise to critical reflection in genre and regionalization. The construction of a Mediterranean "culture area," with its defining traits (e.g., "honour and shame") has been subject to scrutiny, not least by authors whose sphere of interest falls within that geographic region. Most prominently, Herzfeld (1984, 1987) has devoted considerable attention to the "literary" traditions and themes that have been used to construct the "Mediterranean" and "Greece"; see also Galt (1985) on the question of the "Mediterranean." Nevertheless, the "Mediterranean" is an anthropological area that has received a fair measure of attention in the critical evaluation of anthropology and its writing. The Mediterranean has its characteristic, genre-identifying traits—most notably "honour and shame"— that form the leitmotiv for its texts and define its "otherness." Herzfeld's work on the construction of Greece and Hellenism provides an outstanding review of the literature; he explores the rhetoric of anthropological accounts of Greece, together with the attempts of Greeks themselves to define Hellenism. Despite, or perhaps because of, its marginalization, the anthropology of the Mediterranean provides a microcosm of anthropology and its discontents. For similar issues on "Celts"—also absent from Fardon—see McDonald (1989) and Cunningham (1987).

It is not surprising to discover that anthropologists, having incorporated a textual perspective on their discipline, should consider "region" and "genre" together. By the same token, therefore, the relative neglect of this issue by sociologists may be unsurprising, but regrettable for all that. It is easy to treat "ethnography" as a genre in its own right, and for many purposes it is a useful categorization. Yet there are clear textual traditions and conventions that have produced genres and types within the discipline of sociology. Hitherto there has been little systematic attempt to map and describe the varieties. That task is beyond the scope of this book. It requires a monograph in its own right. Nevertheless, some brief observations are essayed here.

One of the most enduring ethnographic traditions—and myths—is the Chicago school of urban sociology (Bulmer, 1984; Harvey, 1987). We know from various sources that there were literary parallels and influences in the development of ethnographic writing in Chicago. The stylistic conventions of realist fiction exerted their influence on the formats of early Chicago ethnography. It was, too, a "regionalizing" genre, in that the city itself was both context and subject-matter for the genre. The city of Chicago is, therefore, one of those urban settings that has taken on an archetypal significance, in a manner similar to some anthropological research sites.

There remains opportunity and need for the textual analysis of the Chicago corpus: *How* have the enduring images of Chicago been produced? Did the massive output of urban sociology in the city consistently reproduce specific, partial versions of Chicago? What were the guiding tropes that shaped the ethnographer's accounts? Analysis along these lines will explore the metaphorical characterization of the city: Thrasher's romantic imagery of "the jungle"; Hughes's metaphor of the organism; the repeated spatial metaphors of the "frontier"; the classic characterization of concentric "zones"; and so on. The reader who works through the monographs will be struck by the stylistic devices used by author after author. The "city" is introduced and anatomised street by street, block by block almost. Readers will find themselves repeatedly retracing the same routes. The student of Chicago sociology cannot fail to become familiar with these characteristic trails. Each of the authors takes the reader along the main thoroughfares that demarcate the "natural areas." The texts of urban exploration are enclosed in the lists of streets, parks, and blocks that map out the city's physiognomy. The reader of Chicago sociology will repeatedly have traversed the same streets: Dearborn, Van Buren, State. They return again and again to "The Loop" and other familiar haunts.

The "point of view" of the classic Chicago ethnographies is a mobile one. The observer and the reader come and go through the streets and the neighbourhoods, noting the sights and the inhabitants, but rarely coming to rest at any one point. In sharp contrast is the "street corner" genre of urban ethnography. At first sight the two varieties of urban sociology are very similar. Indeed, they have much content in common. But the street corner study writes a different version of the urban scene. It is rooted in one locale—the street, the block, the corner. The "city" is a different reality, and the texts introduce and explore their subject-matter very differently. The very names of the ethnographies capture this aspect of the genre: *Street Corner Society* (Whyte, 1981); *The Street Where I Lived* (Williams, 1981); *Tally's Corner* (Liebow, 1967); *Hard Living on Clay Street* (Howell, 1973); *A Place on the Corner* (Anderson, 1978); *Hunter's Point* (Hippler, 1974). In works such as these the "localization" and the thematic emphases of the genre are subtly but fundamentally different from the early studies.

Each genre introduces and locates the observer and the reader in contrasting ways. The early Chicago monograph traverses the city *along* the streets and *between* them. The perspective is that of the walking tour. Although the text is firmly located in the city, it never quite comes to rest. It is not necessarily anchored in a single time and place. By contrast, the "street corner" ethnography places the observer and the reader together in a very specific *spot*. The gaze is not the wandering, planetary scrutiny of the Chicago explorer; it is the intimate and localized view of the narrator "on the spot." Whereas the early Chicago monograph typically introduces the variegated urban vistas of streets, neighbourhoods, quarters, and their teeming inhabitants, the latter genre typically introduces its theme by an autobiographical location of the research. Authors in the style of Liebow or Anderson characteristically tell us how they came to be *there*, and why they stayed there. Reader and ethnographer together are brought into direct and immediate proximity with one another and with the physical location itself. Hammersley (1991) has used Hannerz (1969) to illustrate a similar point. In the monograph *Soulside* the author uses an autobiographical style to locate the reader and the narrator together at a particular spot (Winston St., Washington, D.C.). The descriptive introduction includes particulars that precisely delineate a locale for the research, simultaneously establishing it as a recognizably typical run-down urban scene. Hence, in the two sub-types, the "urban" is constructed quite differently. The "city" is not "the same thing" in each kind of text. In each case, the urban setting is represented by means of synecdoche (that is, the whole is implied through the representation of parts). Each style selects and displays different parts to stand for the urban whole.

Chicago and other U.S. cities do not, of course, furnish the only examples of localized genres. In Britain too there have been several such stylistic and empirical traditions associated with specific locales or localizing strategies. One may turn to the tradition of "community" studies (which are, of course, not exclusively British) and recognize the archetypal position of settings such as the East End of London. Bethnal Green achieved the status of *the* working-class urban community in Britain, redolent with powerful imagery derived from scholarly and popular writing. It is interesting, incidentally, that no British city has been the scene of sociological endeavour and mythology like Chicago. The Institute of Community Studies made a small part of London its focus, but there has not been a consistent tradition of "London" urban sociology. Likewise, the other major cities of the British Isles have hosted studies, but little has emerged as a "localized" genre. We do not have a sociological composite textual picture of, say, Glasgow (for all its images and connotations), or Cardiff (for all the mythology of "Tiger Bay"), or Manchester (for all the legacy of Engels, or the individual modern studies in sociology and anthropology).

The written reconstruction of London's East End provided a highly successful locus classicus for the "written community." Like the *differentia specifica* of anthropology's culture areas, the East Londoners were made to provide the traits of a "traditional" working class. The recurrent themes of extended kinship, matrifocal families, dense exchange networks of mutual obligation were the equivalent of the anthropologists' defining traits of "distinctiveness" and "otherness" (Young & Wilmott, 1957). The East End has continued to exert that kind of imaginative and textual influence, if only in a negative sense. Cornwell's study of family and health in the same area addresses the mythologizing of the earlier monographs, and reorders the romantic themes and images into *one* of the versions available to the local dwellers. They themselves can mythologize their past with reference to a romantic and idealized imagery of "community." But equally they can construct alternative accounts and images of their everyday circumstances that contradict those romantic responses (Cornwell, 1984). Most recently, Hobbs's account again trades on a strongly *localized* sense of the East End of London, which resonates with and resists various of the "traditional" images and constructions of the genre (Hobbs, 1988).

This is not to suggest that British writing is unaffected by matters of genre. Far from it. If specifically local or regional genres are relatively sparse, other dimensions of genre and intertextuality are powerful. For a strong tradition of ethnographic writing exists in which intersect themes of class and region. The author of urban sociology or anthropology in modern Britain can scarcely if ever have escaped some influence of class-imagery from scholarly, literary, and other sources. The writing of working-class "community" their social organization and values, has been an important element in realist fiction, documentary reportage, and the social sciences. The "community" and "the street," whether as Mass Observation's "Worktown," as "Ship Street," or as "The Classic Slum," provide precedent and imagery for all contemporary and subsequent authors. There are, of course, many affinities with North American studies of, say, the urban community or ghetto. But the sense of class continuities is, hardly surprisingly, stronger in the British genre than in the American, which is more preoccupied with a sense of place. Each trades on a sense of "the other" and of "differences." In the North American texts, each locality is identified in terms of its distinctive separation from other localities (often in terms of ethnicity as well as territorial boundaries); the British texts trade rather in the complex differences of class and its subdivisions. The British are typically more concerned with the fine gradations of inter- and intra-class differences, but the American authors are equally likely to construct their arguments in terms of the cultural specificity of their chosen locale. Here, for instance, Suttles's work on the social order of the "slum" is a type-case: he emphasises the importance of the "local culture" in explaining continuity and stability, even as he emphasises the territorial and ethnic segmentation of his chosen "field" (Suttles, 1968).

There are other notable dimensions of genre differentiation. They include generational differences within intellectual fields, which are closely linked to theoretical and methodological variations. Although there are important continuities within the ethnographic tradition, there are changes over time as well. Many "classic" ethnographies look oddly dated when compared with contemporary examples. Few authors today would expect to "get away with" the style of early Chicago monographs (landmarks though they were). The global, generalized account has given way to more specific and selective accounts. Within specialized fields of study the style and subject-matter shift subtly but significantly. Van Maanen (personal communication, 1990) notes concerning his own field of police studies "first generation police researchers hitting hard the violence, duplicity, racist themes of urban policing; the second generation hitting the mundane, routine, workaday themes; the third generation hitting the internal variability themes; and the context specificity of previously held generalizations." Changing focus reflects theoretical and methodological development. Each new style reflects each generation's demarcation of its new, special, even unique, contribution.

A genre, whether it be a localized or a thematic one, or one derived primarily from a disciplinary and theoretical perspective, is a powerful framework within which each ethnography is read and written. As various authors have suggested, intellectual traditions are marked and characterized by their own distinctive written products. When we encounter any given ethnography, we find work that reflects a number of antecedents and influences. It is not necessary for the author to be aware of them consciously. (For analytic purposes in reading those texts, the author's awareness or understanding may be largely irrelevant; for the development of critical and reflexive scholarship, it may be more important). There are different generic traditions that may impinge on the production of the text: the discipline, the theoretical orientation, the subject-matter all play their part. The ethnographer, unless consciously manipulating or experimenting with style, is likely to write in a way that seems "natural" or "appropriate," and in doing so will draw on prior reading in the field, the instruction and example of mentors, the reputation of classic texts. In that sense, therefore, the ethnography is thoroughly "intertextual." Its account of *its* social world is mediated by other ethnographic accounts of *other* social worlds. Each author brings to the ethnographic task his or her reading of "the literature," as well as a personal style, and the particular experience of "the field." Each monograph (or indeed any text) is a kind of *bricolage*. The disciplinary and generic themes and elements are reassembled and deployed by each individual author.

The same issues impinge, of course, on the *reading* of ethnographic texts. It is a commonplace to assert that reading is active, and that the "reception" of a text is the outcome of the reader's interpretation of what is read. That cannot mean, however, that there is a completely indeterminate relationship between the text and its reception, any more than it renders "the author" entirely redundant for all practical and theoretical purposes. Readers and writers together share (to varying degrees, admittedly) cultural knowledge and values that inform production and reception alike. That is especially evident when we are dealing with an epistemic collectivity such as an academic discipline. It is reasonable to assume that even though each individual scholar's stock of expert knowledge of texts is unique, nonetheless, readers and writers of ethnographies in the same research domain have a high level of shared understanding. Consequently, when I read an ethnography for the first time, I am not a naive reader. I read in the light of my—largely tacit—understanding of the relevant conventions and practices. I use my aesthetic judgements—which again are often implicit—to compare the text with others I have read in the same vein. There is, therefore, a complex web of reading and writing relations that construct our understanding of "the ethnography"—and hence of the social world.

6. ALTERNATIVES

Practitioners of the humane disciplines, including the social sciences, cannot any longer be innocent about their writing. It is integral to our contemporary (the confusing terminology precludes "modern") intellectual state that the textuality of representation is itself problematic. We have become increasingly aware of the extent to which texts—be they "fiction" or "fact," "prose" or "poetry," "literature" or "science"—are all *conventional*. Language is not a transparent medium through which the world may be experienced or expressed. Neither speech nor writing can furnish a privileged, neutral mechanism of representation. Rather, language is always "incomplete." It does not give us an exhaustive description of the physical and social world. However "factual" or "realistic" a text appears to be, it is inescapably dependent on the conventions of reading and writing that its producer and consumers bring to bear.

We have been forced to recognize that reading is an active pursuit. The reader *makes* sense of the text, reading *into* it more than it can state in so many words. That view comes as no surprise to the good ethnographer: it is almost a commonplace among cultural anthropologists, symbolic inter-actionists, or ethnomethodologists. The interpretive or hermeneutic tendency in sociology and anthropology has roots in diverse philosophical, theoretical, and methodological inspirations. Nevertheless, it has a shared commitment to the fundamental, but problematic character of meaning. It recognizes that "the meaning" of spoken or written language is not fixed "in the words." Meaning is not static, but processual and emergent out of the interaction between speaker and hearer, or between reader and text.

There are various contemporary intellectual currents that contribute to this self-conscious awareness of the work of representation: hermeneutics, post-structuralism, postmodernism. It is not the task of this short book to review all those theoretical currents. No attempt will even be made to define them, for the definitions and uses of the terms are highly variable from one discipline to another, or even from one commentator to another. Moreover, although some scholars find intellectual inspiration eclectically from several such theoretical tendencies, others find the various positions antithetical and incompatible. Rather than trying to define and pin down the flux of contemporary ideas, I find it more useful to outline and explore how those ideas have impinged upon the ethnographic imagination in sociology and anthropology. Several of the themes have already informed this discussion. They include a radical questioning of the certainty and authority of the scholarly text; a rejection of the search for "truth" and reason as absolutes; a denial of the intellectual and moral distance between the academic and his or her human "subjects"; a suspicion of the "big" narratives of totalizing theory (historical, Marxist, sociological). The positive emphases lead to a preference for texts that are "playful" and fragmented. The "serious" search for the meaning hidden beneath the text is replaced by an eclectic assimilation of pastiche, irony, and "surface" style. One should note, however, that pastiche is not a recent phenomenon. Duff (1935) produced a spoof anthropological report on a London suburb, supposedly penned by Professor Vladimir Chernichewski, prior to his departure for new fieldwork on the island of Capri.

The impact of these and similar ideas on anthropology has been startling. It is evident that they have informed a contemporary crisis in the discipline—especially, but not exclusively, in U.S. cultural anthropology. Here, for the critics at least, was a discourse that above all celebrated the dichotomies and the certainties of "modernity." For all its cultural relativizing, anthropology could appear as the prime example of scholarly writing in which the intellectual and moral authority of the observer was assured, in contrast to the object of the ethnographic gaze. For over a decade now anthropologists have been reflecting, even agonizing, over their intellectual predicament (Spencer, 1989).

Anthropological discourse implicitly asserts the triumph of the modern, and of the West—it is argued—by its implicit claim to privilege. In one sense modern anthropology shares something with "postmodernism." It was born of a renunciation of the grand narratives of nineteenth-century scholarship. Its founders (the heroes once, but now sometimes the villains of its origin myths) preferred the small-scale, the local, the synchronic—the small narratives—to the great overarching schemata of evolutionary social theory and the encyclopaedic classification of human societies. The idiographic description of societies and cultures supplemented or replaced the nomothetic ideal. Yet modern anthropology, the critics maintain, carried with it the textual practices and intellectual styles of the grand narrative based on the dichotomies of "us" and "the other." The alien, the exotic may lose its "savage" and "primitive" connotations, and yet remain the strange and unknown terrain that awaits "discovery" and exploration by the West.

The critique has come from various sources. The history of the ethnographic gaze has been pushed back in time. Whereas once the histories began and ended with the major figures of this century—Malinowski, Boas, and their immediate circles—now the history is coterminous with "the modern" era more generally. Hence Todorov (1984) writes of the "discovery" of the Americas by Europeans and the construction of its inhabitants as "other." Likewise Said's influential work recounts the discursive production of "the Orient" in the Near East and Middle East by the surveys and explorations of Western Europeans (Said, 1978). "Orientalism," in Said's usage, is the frame of mind and the textual practice whereby "otherness" is fixed and "the other" appropriated. The root metaphors remain: the silent and unknown is given voice by the ethnographer who speaks for the other.

The encounter between Ethnographer and Alter, from this perspective, is not a dialogue. The ethnographer's is the dominant voice. The ethnography is determined by the "point of view" of the ethnographer. For all the interpretation of "the natives" and their accounts, the monograph remains what Bakhtin (e.g., 1981) called "monologic": it is dominated by the voice of the privileged narrator. The attitude of mind and the texts it produces are "contemplative": the ethnographer is effaced and detached from the object of inquiry. The critique of "conventional" ethnography therefore interweaves the analysis and interpretation of its texts with more general ideological and epistemological reservations. The "ethnography" of the self-confident discipline in its hey-day inscribes the moral and intellectual perspective of classical anthropology. The textual analysis of ethnographic discourse in cultural and social anthropology is therefore a symptom of a profound malaise that has assailed the academy. The encounter with the "Other" renders anthropology the most obvious and fertile terrain for this contemporary critique of representation. It is by no means the only one: indeed, all the human disciplines are susceptible to critical reflection of the same sort.

The representation of the "Other" in ethnographic texts is now a thoroughly pervasive feature of anthropology: a commonplace as Dwyer (1982) puts it. McGrane (1989) is among the authors to have traced the history of "The Other" in the literature. He describes how "the other" was constructed in three successive intellectual epochs. Each produced the contrast of "difference" in accordance with different criteria. In Renaissance discourse, the relevant moral and intellectual framework was religious. The non-European alien was coded in terms of the "pagan," "heathen," and the demonic. For the Enlightenment, the key feature of the other was "ignorance" and "superstition." In the nineteenth century, when modern anthropology was born, the "primitive" was coded in terms of "development" and evolutionary time.

There are, of course, many consequences of this critique of "modern" high ethnography. They are political, ethical, and epistemological. In the eyes of many recent observers they constitute a profound threat to the discipline of anthropology itself. On all sides the subject is described as finding itself in a state of crisis. In contrast, sociology has felt the implications of recent and contemporary intellectual currents without the same sense of crisis. Perhaps that is because the discipline never had the self-assurance of anthropology; it has been for many years characterized by theoretical and methodological pluralism and contention. The claims of poststructuralism, postmodernism, and the like have not been felt as an assault on a previously secure edifice.

The implications of postmodern critique go well beyond the scope of this book. They are important, however, in that they have consequences for the reading and writing of ethnography. There have been several responses to the critique of conventional ethnographic representations. The surface of the text has become more fragmented and more diverse; there is an emphasis on "dialogic" forms of representation; elements of parody and pastiche have been allowed to enter the intellectual field. The scholarly text has itself become a more "open" one, repudiating the closure and certainty of the orthodox work.

The fragmented text avoids those representational devices whereby "the culture" is captured and contained within a single narrative that is reconstructed by one single voice, from a single point of view. If culture itself is seen as fragmentary and incoherent, then the texts of its representation may appropriately be likewise. The ethnographer can no longer subordinate all of his or her "data" to unifying themes and models. The work of the text is more overtly recognized as an act of *bricolage*: the fragments of "data" (which are themselves crafted rather than found) are thus juxtaposed. The textual arrangement therefore becomes a kind of "collage" or, as Dorst (1989) calls his work, an "assemblage." Dorst's is an avowedly postmodern ethnography that attempts to deal with postmodern cultural phenomena. Writing of a suburban site—Chadds Ford—Dorst collects together various fragments that he refers to as "souvenirs" of the setting. The various memorabilia and noteworthy sights there collected recapitulate how Chadds Ford is itself created. There is a process of "auto-ethnography": the "reality" of the place is itself derived from its various representations and simulacra. In what he describes as "post-ethnographic practice" Dorst seeks to minimize his own interpretation and exegeses. Even where his authorial voice appears, Dorst immediately seeks to disarm: "In keeping with the general premise of this study though, when interpretive commentary drops in it should be read as just another textual fragment of the same order as the souvenirs, another item in the collection" (p. 5). In a similar vein, Rose's text (1989) is an instance of how the self-consciously "postmodern" ethnography adopts a highly fragmented and variegated textual format. In the space of one very brief monograph he touches on a diverse range of themes and topics: from historical sources on the colonization of America, to poems, autobiographical fragments, extracts from an ethnographic project among black people in South Philadelphia, set alongside accounts of scenes from corporate life and of cultural entrepreneurship. (Rose's writing takes him via the Brandywine

River and Chadds Ford, as does Dorst's: perhaps the locale and its inhabitants are to become icons or archetypes in the canon of postmodern ethnographic studies). The entries from Rose's journals are not deployed as "data" in the more "conventional" ethnographic formats: they are distributed among the various other textual fragments and brief essays. The effects of the text are derived from the contrasts and juxtapositions rather than from a sense of cumulative evidence, unfolding narrative, or logical progression. Within the compass of a very short monograph, the focus shifts repeatedly, as does the style of writing itself.

The fragmentation of the text is endorsed in the search for "dialogic" modes of representation. The position here is exemplified by Dwyer's work in Morocco (1982). Dwyer rejects what he regards as many of the assumptions and root metaphors of anthropology: the contemplative ethnography through which the Self confronts and objectifies the Other; the search for the pristine, exotic Other; the transformation of the fieldwork encounter into the idealized conjuncture of archetypal Self and Other. In contrast to the standard presentational formats of anthropology and sociology, the bulk of Dwyer's "monograph" consists of a series of dialogues between himself and a Moroccan Faqir—a cultivator in his mid-60s. The "dialogues" are collected and presented under the rubric of a "record" of fieldwork. Dwyer insists that "The Other" shall have a voice. The text is not the product of one dominant voice. Rather, both become active subjects in the encounter. Of the fieldwork record that constitutes the first part of the book Dwyer claims:

> In the personal confrontation between Self and Other, the barrier between the two is broken down as the parties interact, daily, with one another; also the illusion of an objective Self becomes untenable, because more participation in the confrontation inevitably locates the self culturally as the "outsider" intruding on the Other's terrain, and historically as a representative of a society that has a prior history of intrusion. (p. 274)

The book thus consists primarily of transcribed conversations between the two men. The anthropologist's voice is heard as an interlocutor, not as commentator or analyst. Dwyer argues that the reproduction of the dialogues as the fieldwork record preserves the encounter between the anthropologist and "informant," in which the "meaning" of the talk is recognized as emergent and contingent. Dwyer contrasts his own mode of presentation with those of other authors who employ apparently similar modes of representation. He argues that even when anthropologists have focused their attention on conversations in the field, they have done so in a way that underplays the differences between the Self and the Other: in the accounts as published, they "transcend their differences" and "become transparent to one another" (p. 276). Dwyer, for instance, contrasts his own textual practices and commitments with those of such well-known authors as Rabinow (1977) and Crapanzano (1980). For instance, of Crapanzano's conversations with Tuhami, Dwyer notes that Tuhami's words are reproduced only in short extracts, rather than transcribed in extenso, and Crapanzano feels free to interpolate summary statements of Tuhami's beliefs and of a generalized Moroccan culture. Crapanzano's subsequent work, published after Dwyer's account, seems to go towards the other extreme: his white South African informants' accounts are reconstructed as extensive autobiographical narratives. But Dwyer's other stricture still applies, in that the "Self" of Crapanzano is absent. The informants speak, but there is no voice of the anthropologist prompting and questioning. The accounts still lack the discursive context within which they and their meanings were produced.

The thoroughly dialogic approach does not take the fragmentary nature of the data of "interviews," "dialogues" (or whatever the encounters are to be called) and transform them into tidier categories and collections. It preserves the sense of exploration and the precariously provisional nature of mutual understanding. The textual presentation of Dwyer's dialogues preserves a paradox, however. The transcription of the conversations captures the extent to which Dwyer's data collection consisted *not* in conversational "dialogues," so much as in *interrogations*. There seems no qualitative difference between the talk between Dwyer and the Faqir and the content of most conventional research interviewing. Dwyer's interviewing strategy at times seems like a clear exemplification of Spradley's methodological advice for ethnographic interviewing (Spradley, 1979). The author, to be fair, recognizes the issue at one point in his introductory passages:

> The events and dialogues illustrate the structured inequality of the partners during their encounter: the anthropologist singles out "events" and poses questions; the informant answers, embellishes, digresses, evades. The anthropologist, in part for reasons and in a manner reflecting his own society's concerns, is pushed to impose form upon his experience, and his questions provide a skeleton designed to provoke the informant to respond; the informant's responses add flesh to this frame and dress it, often in unexpected ways. (p. xvii)

This acknowledgement does not, however, prevent Dwyer entering some far-reaching claims for the reproduction of his transcribed conversations with his informant. In the event, it is doubtful whether a major "postmodern" practice can really be sustained simply through the reproduction of interviews. The notion of the equivalence of "voices" is not matched by simply providing the transcribed speech of the fieldworker and the informant. Where the "other" is constrained by the interrogative voice of the ethnographer, then the speech exchange does not correspond to the ideal of the "dialogic." It is, indeed, ironic to reflect that the interrogative strategies employed in Dwyer's interviews with the Faqir, and celebrated by him for their revelatory power, would in other contexts be treated quite differently. The question-and-answer sequences, when translated to other contexts such as the doctor's surgery or the school classroom, would normally be found to be enactments of domination and control. One is reminded, for instance, of Mishler's analysis of medical discourse: in the interrogative mode of the medical history-taking, the "voice" of medicine *interrupts* the patient's "voice" of the life-world (Mishler, 1984). This is not a "dialogue." In the same way, in the Moroccan transcripts the voice of the anthropologist interrupts the voice of the everyday world of the Faqir.

My interest here is not to enter too far into a critique of Dwyer's version of "postmodernism." The point is rather to note how that epistemological commitment can lead to one sort of textual practice. The intellectual crisis of anthropology gives rise to texts in which the authority and superiority of the author give way to a variety of reticence. The "meaning" and the "culture" are to be constructed *by* the reader, rather than being constructed *for* the reader by the implied narrator. The same sort of inspiration is to be found in the work of Tyler (1987) and of Dumont (1978). As Tyler puts it, postmodern ethnography "privileges 'discourse' over 'text,' it foregrounds dialogue as opposed to monologue, and emphasizes the cooperative and collaborative nature of the ethnographic situation" (p. 203). And to some degree, Dumont's monograph is a concrete expression of that ideal. The ethnographic process is represented as a dialogue between the two individuals ("The Headman" and "I"). The emphasis throughout is on the collaborative negotiation of the ethnography through the fieldwork encounter.

It is congruent with the general aesthetic and intellectual movement of postmodernism that the forms of parody and pastiche should increasingly find their place in scholarly writing. The taken-for-granted distinction between "serious" and "playful" writing is dissolved in the hands of some recent writers. Their approach is eclectic. The fragmentation of the textual surface is achieved by a mixing of styles and genres within the same text, or within the same corpus. There is a deliberate transgression of literary boundaries; a promiscuous mingling of modes.

The most consistent programme of textual experimentation in that vein has been launched by sociologists of science. A network of authors has established various "alternative" literary modes for the construction of their sociological texts. (They are not necessarily referred to as derived from "ethnographic" research, but qualitative data collection strategies such as extended interviewing with key informants underpins the work). In a series of startling and often amusing texts the authors construct non-traditional accounts, based on "literary" models such as the short story or one-act play. Rather than the single "voice" or point of view of a single authorial stance, the textual formats allow for a range of different perspectives or positions to be "voiced" in the one text. The text's surface is therefore fragmented in the sense that a dialogue or argument is enacted. The form of the philosophical "dialogue" is an apt parallel. (This is different from the dialogic mode advocated by Dwyer, Fabian, and others: the dialogues of the alternative literary forms do not report the transactions of fieldwork, but contrive reconstructed or invented exchanges between real or imaginary speakers).

Mulkay (1985) has provided the intellectual inspiration for this self-conscious experimentation with literary forms. As well as exemplifying the approach in his various papers on the sociology of scientific knowledge, Mulkay has offered explicit advocacy for a self-conscious attention to literary forms. His empirical work is best known among sociologists of science. It deserves to be known by all sociologists and anthropologists who are seriously interested in the possibilities of textual form and representation, irrespective of their substantive interests. His book—part methodological, part epistemological, part empirical—is self-referential. In advocating alternative literary forms, Mulkay employs them from the outset. The work is introduced through a dialogue between the author and the reader; a third voice, "the book," introduces itself. Mulkay goes on to use various textual devices to develop his explorations of scientific knowledge and discourse. One chapter, for instance, takes the form of a one-act play. An analysis of experimental replication in science is developed through a fictional exchange between a laboratory scientist and two sociologists of science (a U.S. female and British male), while yet a third (female) sociologist passes through, briefly, wielding her tape-recorder. The device allows Mulkay to confront two contrasting views of sociology with the conventional wisdom of the laboratory scientist. In a similar vein, Mulkay explores the analytic issue of what counts as a scientific "discovery" through an imaginary discourse. The participants to the discussion include several scientific "types," a young sociologist (named and modelled after an actual figure) and an "auditor." (The irony of the piece includes the presence of an auditor to inquire into a discovery when, as Mulkay explains, "a genuine auditor's job is to discover whether there was a fraud and, if so, who is to be held responsible for it" [p. 202].) The results of these inventions can be both illuminating and amusing. The humorous effect is perhaps most apparent in Mulkay's "analytical parody" based on the Nobel Prize ceremony. In a fictional version, the participants' speeches are made to subvert the ceremonial requirements of the event. By constructing what is not normally said and what is normally left unsaid, Mulkay highlights the conventional form and content of scientific "noblesse oblige." As with all Mulkay's inventions, the fictional versions are put together out of fragments of "real" utterances and exchanges. As with all "analyses," the texts are arranged and constructed by the author out of shards of evidence. The difference between conventional ethnographic accounts and Mulkay's literary inventions is not a hard-and-fast separation between the factual and the fictional. Mulkay's are notable because the analyst *explicitly* claims the right to fashion the materials into new arrangements and to mould them into a range of different formats.

Throughout Mulkay's textual inventions there is a constant recognition that the original "data" are themselves "textual" products. In other words, the sociologist's "subjects" or "informants" themselves use various rhetorical or textual formats through which they fashion their accounts of the world and their actions. Mulkay is not, therefore, simply interested in "making up" his own "fictional" versions; rather, he uses his rhetorical skills to explore the textual productions of social actors *and* sociologists. Consequently, Mulkay argues, the work of the social scientist is to construct "secondary" texts that use and build on the "original" texts of everyday life. In that the secondary texts are necessarily different from the "original" ones, rather than being a mere recapitulation of them, they may be thought, in principle, to stand in an ironic or parodic relationship to them. The parody is based on the original text, but departs from it and reveals the meaning of the original. In explaining the original text, the parody simultaneously celebrates its own superiority over it.

Mulkay's literary conceits are not, therefore, gratuitous jeux d'esprit. The variety of textual forms, and the repeated juxtapositions of "original" and "fictional" texts constantly bring to consciousness the formal properties of discourse, spoken and written. Throughout, Mulkay's texts subvert the more conventional reliance on the single voice of the analyst: " The analyst's claim of interpretative superiority is ill-founded and ... the nature of conventional, monologic sociological discourse seriously limits the possibility of any helpful practical application of sociological knowledge" (p. 7).

The style has been developed by Mulkay and his collaborators in several works, based primarily on original texts jointly produced in interview talk between sociologists and informants. Here again the primary materials are worked into a variety of different textual formats that allow Mulkay and his collaborators to explore issues of knowledge and discourse from a variety of perspectives. The tone is consistently one of quizzical skepticism: the alternative literary formats such as the dialogue or the play are ideally suited to the exploration of ambiguity and uncertainty. The texts frequently expose inconsistency and juxtapose incompatible positions. The textual devices allow the authors to display these differences without having to impose closure and certainty on the materials.

The variety of textual formats may be deployed within one single study, as in the research on health economics by Ashmore, Mulkay, and Pinch (1989). The monograph is developed through a number of different styles of presentation. In part, the qualitative data are reported "straight": extracts of interview transcripts are used to generate and illustrate a series of analytic themes. At the outset, the unsuspecting reader, unacquainted with the group's previous publications, could probably assume that he or she had set out to read a conventional piece of qualitative reportage. That expectation, and the surface of the text, are disrupted when the authors introduce another textual device. Fragments from mass media coverage of health economies are assembled and opposed, without commentary. (The authors are present in the text, however: they include a fictional piece of journalism in which their work on health economists is reported. It includes an announcement of the publication of the book in which the "report" is reproduced.) The presentation continues through a "dialogue" between "the authors" and a skeptical voice—also, of course, produced by the authors. This is followed by a playlet in five acts, in which the sociologists themselves, three health economists, a tape-recorder and video-recorder are dramatis personae. The sociologists' words are invented; those of the other characters are reproduced verbatim from research texts and transcripts. There are various other witty effects. For instance, from time to time passing reference is made to "Mrs. Jones," who stands for the generalized lay person exercising choice. This lay figure is part of the stock-in-trade of the economist (under various aliases). In this book, "Mrs. Jones" acquires a voice for herself. Ashmore et al. give the last word to Mrs. Jones, who turns round and comments on the self-limiting character of her creators' fictions:

> I got the impression that they were in favour of changing sociology so that the so-called expert's voice didn't dominate so much. I certainly approve of *that*. But *of course* I approve! I'm no more than a textual device of their making. I'm entirely under their control. It seems to me that I'm rather like the economists' rhetoric of nationality, behind which they exercise their own hidden judgements. I'm an illusion of multivocality . . . behind which the sociologists continue to assume their own privileged knowledge of the social world. So I think we need one more paradox: that social scientists can only claim to speak on our behalf by refusing to let us speak for ourselves. I think we'll call this the "paradox of applied social science." (p. 208)

Similar stylistic devices have been used by Mulkay and his collaborators in a number of works on the sociology of scientific knowledge. Indeed, the use of "alternative" literary forms has become recognized as a distinct approach within that network of scholars.

The "literary" forms used by Mulkay are not in themselves "alternative." They are well-established forms put to the rather strange use of conveying sociological analyses. They do not purport to stand in any particular relationship to the subject-matter they report. They are not couched as one-act plays, for instance, because "scientific" discourse is normally reproduced that way. Quite the reverse, in fact: there is a startling discordance between the witty, literary pastiches and the "normal" content of normal science. But at least one author has quite explicitly adopted a form of writing that matches the subject-matter. Moreover, he has provided us with an autobiographical account of how that writing came about. Moeran has written two book-length works based on his fieldwork in Japan (1985, 1990). The first was a standard realist ethnography on the folk-craft potters of Onta. The second was a "fictionalized" version of a field diary (*Okubo Diary*). There is, of course, nothing novel in such a fictionalized version of a fieldworker's experiences. Most famous, perhaps, was Laura Bohannan's *Return to Laughter*, which she published as a work of fiction under a pseudonym (Bowen, 1954). Where Moeran's differs, however, is in his incorporation of *Japanese* literary forms. As he explains it, he drew on a venerable Japanese tradition in which the literary diary is a distinct type (the *nikki* genre). The text is therefore loaded with allusions to classical Japanese literature, and the "literary diary" was allowed to impose its own form on the order and style of the narrative.

Passages are interspersed with short, haiku-like sections, for instance. Moeran's reflections on his text are especially useful, as they include commentary on how the work developed, how the decisions to work in Japanese-influenced style implied further decisions, and how in the process the "fieldnote" journals were transformed into the "fictionalized" literary diary (Moeran, 1990). He reflects on the extent to which it has been transformed in the process, "to what extent is it a 'fieldwork journal' as opposed to a 'literary diary,' and vice-versa" (p. 345). He concludes with an elegant, and entirely appropriate view:

> I have tried to show how the choice of a literary genre, together with the process of writing itself, involved me as a writer in a format that both permitted creativity and imposed constraint. One aspect of creativity discussed here has focused on the degree to which the author is able to fictionalize his or her ethnographic material—by eliding time, by creating composite characters, and by framing minor episodes within larger narrative structures. These fictionalizing processes suggest that it is quite possible for ethnographers to slip from "objective fact" into "subjective fiction" without anyone but the ethnographer being aware of the fact (or fiction, as the case may be). (p. 352)

The strategies of Mulkay and Moeran have important similarities. Both employ self-conscious parodies of "high" literary forms; both "take liberties" with the original materials, which are reordered, reattributed, used to make fictional narratives out of actual events and utterances. The effects are startling and engaging: the reader is aware of the form, which resists the taken-for-granted reading of most conventionally "realist" accounts.

There is a marked contrast between the "postmodern" manifestos of authors such as Tyler and the parodic inventions of a Mulkay. The former tends to produce highly complex and "difficult" texts; the latter's "literary" pieces are highly entertaining and engaging. In Mulkay's hands, the dialogic form is translated into a *readable* text; in Tyler's, the result is a complex, "writerly" product. Both are responses to contemporary sensibilities concerning textuality. Their realizations are very different.

A small number of authors have taken the use of "literary" pastiche and invention to the point where they cease to represent or reconstruct recognizable and plausible social worlds in any conventional sense. Rose, for instance, concludes his book with a strikingly bizarre fantasy or allegory, which is closer to science fiction and is certainly far removed from conventional realist writing. It is one extreme implication of the licence claimed by some contemporary authors—as we have seen—to invent and devise with some degree of creative freedom. It celebrates, perhaps, the distinction and the characterization proposed by Tyler (1987). Tyler suggests that the relevant contrast is not between "fact" (ethnography) and "fiction" (literature) but between fiction and "fantasy" (ethnography) so that:

> A postmodern ethnography is a co-operatively evolved text consisting of fragments of discourse intended to evoke in the minds of both reader and writer an emergent fantasy of a possible world of commonsense reality, and thus to provoke an aesthetic integration, that will have a therapeutic effect. (p. 202)

In Tyler's work the term "evocation" is a key one. The goal of evocation liberates ethnography from the false aspirations and dichotomies Tyler finds in conventional approaches.

> The whole point of "evoking" rather than "representing" is that it frees ethnography from mimesis and that inappropriate mode of scientific rhetoric which entails "object," "facts," "descriptions," "inductions," "generalizations," "verification," "experiment," "truth," and like concepts which, except as empty invocations, have no parallels either in the experience of ethnographic fieldwork or in the writing of ethnographies. (p. 207)

It is, of course, a pretty momentous step to claim that one can at a stroke transcend all those issues and concerns that have preoccupied ethnographers (and many others) for so long. As Hobart (1990) points out, there is a degree to which Tyler, and some other "textualists" in the anthropological camp, set up straw arguments. Few anthropologists or sociologists, if any, are wedded to the crude correspondence theory of representation imputed by Tyler above. Few are blithely unaware of the character of language, even though not all carry through their realization to the extreme logical conclusion advocated by Tyler himself.

There is, it appears, a series of problems and paradoxes, limitations and liabilities inherent in the extreme "postmodern" position. There is danger that in rejecting a naive adherence to representation ("mimesis") as unproblematic, the texts lose all sense of reference to a social world, but become overwhelmingly *self*-referential. The problems arise if a particular insight or innovation is taken to extremes. Indeed, if it is not too much of an oxymoron, some authors take this understanding of the non-literal character of language far too literally!

7. CONCLUSION

Ethnographers, like many contemporary scholars, have become increasingly preoccupied with the nature and consequences of their textual practices. This short monograph is part of a rapidly growing literature. There is no doubt that sociologists, anthropologists, and others have gained considerable insight into their own craft through reflection on the texts of their discipline. There has, however, been much heat generated as well as light, and some arguments based on rhetorical, poststructuralist, or postmodern criticism have been taken to extremes.

Some commentators have become so obsessively focused on "text" that they are prepared to deny or overlook any referential value for academic writing. From the point of view of the extreme "textualist," ethnographic writing refers to itself and to other texts. It does not report a social world that is independent of its textual representations. There is no mimetic function. From this point of view, "realism" is only a mode of writing. It is important to note therefore that the position taken in this book does not correspond to that extreme. The social world is not confined to the texts that purport to describe it, and the two should not be confused.

In the foregoing sections I have outlined a number of ways in which "readable" accounts of the social world are produced and received. I have also indicated some of the ways in which more "writerly" versions have been essayed. I have discussed some of the methods by which the authors and readers of ethnography draw on common conventions to make aspects of social life understandable. Those strategies are all based on conventional practices of reading and writing. But we should not and need not therefore assume that they have no capacity to represent and reveal aspects of the social world. The ethnographer is undoubtedly an artisan who crafts narratives and representations. But it is an illicit sleight of hand to refer to their products as "fictions," just because they are "made." It is equally misleading to exploit the two connotations of "artefact": our work is a human creation, but is not necessarily the equivalent of a spurious measurement or finding. All our human capacities for symbolic activity are based on conventional and arbitrary signs and their interrelationships. That does not, however, rob them of practical value. We use them to interact with the world and with one another. If we recognize the rhetorical and even the aesthetic foundations of our work, then we must not forget the pragmatic bases of our investigations.

It would therefore be quite wrong for a reader of this book to leave it with the view that there is "nothing beyond the text." Such a view recapitulates the mistaken separation of Science and Rhetoric. It was wrong to celebrate science and ignore rhetoric. It is equally wrong simply to reverse the emphasis. Scholarship is rhetorical in the sense that its arguments are shaped, illustrated, and explained to audiences of readers. Its practitioners must use the methods of representation that are to hand. But that is not a dispensation for irresponsibility. On the contrary, just as the researcher must take responsibility for theoretical and methodological decisions, so textual or representational decisions must be made responsibly. We do not have perfect theoretical and epistemological foundations; we do not have perfect methods for data collection; we do not have perfect or transparent modes of representation. We work in the knowledge of our limited resources. But we do not have to abandon the attempt to produce disciplined accounts of the world that are coherent, methodical, and sensible. The purpose of this book has been to contribute to our general understanding of the choices and consequences that must be addressed in the reading and writing of ethnographic work.

REFERENCES

Adam, B. (1990). *Time and social theory.* Cambridge, UK: Polity.

Anderson, E. (1978). *A place on the corner.* Chicago: University of Chicago Press.

Ankersmit, F. R. (1983). *Narrative logic: A semantic analysis of the historian's language.* The Hague: Nijhoff.

Ashmore, M., Mulkay, M., & Pinch, T. (1989). *Health and efficiency: A sociology of health economics.* Milton Keynes, UK: Open University Press.

Atkinson, P. (1981). *The clinical experience: The construction and reconstruction of medical reality.* Aldershot, UK: Gower

Atkinson, P. (1982). Writing ethnography. In H. J. Helle (Ed.), *Kultur und Institution* (pp. 77-105). Berlin: Dunker und Humblot.

Atkinson, P. (1990). *The ethnographic imagination: Textual constructions of reality.* London: Routledge.

Atkinson, P. (1991). Supervising the text. *International Journal of Qualitative Studies in Education, 4,* 161-174.

Bakhtin, M. M. (1981). *The dialogic imagination.* Austin: University of Texas Press.

Barthes, R. (1974). *S/Z.* New York: Hill and Wang.

Bazerman, C. (1988). *Shaping written knowledge: The genre and the activity of the experimental article in science.* Madison: University of Wisconsin Press.

Becker, H. S. (1986). *Writing for social scientists.* Chicago: University of Chicago Press.

Billig, M. (1987). *Arguing and thinking: A rhetorical approach to social psychology.* Cambridge, UK: Cambridge University Press.

Blumer, H. (1954). What's wrong with social theory? *American Sociological Review, 19,* 3-10.

Bond, G. C. (1990). Fieldnotes: Research in past occurrence. In P. Sanjek (Ed.), *Fieldnotes: The makings of anthropology* (pp. 273-289). Ithaca, NY: Cornell University Press.

Boon, J. A. (1982). *Other tribes, other scribes: Symbolic anthropology in the comparative study of cultures, histories, religions and texts.* Cambridge, UK: Cambridge University Press.

Boon, J. A. (1983). Functionalists write too: Frazer, Malinowski and the semiotics of the monograph. *Semiotica, 46*(2-4), 131-149.

Bourdieu, P., & Passeron, J.-C. (1977). *Reproduction in education, society and culture.* London: Sage.

Bowen, E. (1954). *Return to laughter.* London: Gollancz.

Brown, R. H. (1977). *A poetic for sociology.* Cambridge, UK: Cambridge University Press.

Brown, R. H. (1987). *Society as text: Essays on rhetoric, reason and reality.* Chicago: University of Chicago Press.

Bulmer, M. (1984). *The Chicago school of sociology.* Chicago: University of Chicago Press.

Clifford, J. (1988). *The predicament of culture.* Cambridge, MA: Harvard University Press.

Clifford, J. (1990). Notes on (field)notes. In R. Sanjek (Ed.), *Fieldnotes: The makings of anthropology* (pp. 47-70). Ithaca, NY: Cornell University Press.

Clifford, J., & Marcus, G. E. (Eds.). (1986). *Writing culture.* Berkeley: University of California Press.

54

Cooper, D. E. (1984). Labov, Larry and Charles. *Oxford Review of Education, 10,* 177-192.

Cornwell, J. (1984). *Hard-earned lives: Accounts of health and illness from East London.* London: Tavistock.

Coser, L. (1974). *Greedy institutions.* New York: Free Press.

Crapanzano, V. (1977). The writing of ethnography. *Dialectical Anthropology, 2,* 69-73.

Crapanzano, V. (1980). *Tuhami: Portrait of a Moroccan.* Chicago: University of Chicago Press.

Crapanzano, V. (1986). *Waiting: The whites of South Africa.* London: Paladin.

Cunningham, R. (1987). *Apples on the flood: The Southern Mountain experience.* Knoxville: University of Tennessee Press.

Delamont, S. (1981). All too familiar? *Educational Analysis, 3,* 69-83.

Dorst, J. D. (1989). *The written suburb: An ethnographic dilemma.* Philadelphia: University of Pennsylvania Press.

Duff, C. (1935). *Anthropological report on a London suburb.* London: Grayson and Grayson.

Dumont, J. P. (1978). *The headman and I.* Austin: University of Texas Press.

Dwyer, K. (1982). *Moroccan dialogues: Anthropology in question.* Baltimore, MD: Johns Hopkins University Press. (Reissued 1987, Prospect Heights, IL: Waveland Press)

Edmondson, R. (1984). *Rhetoric in sociology.* London: Macmillan.

Fabian, J. (1983). *Time and the other: How anthropology makes its object.* New York: Columbia University Press.

Fardon, R. (1990a). Localising strategies: The regionalisation of ethnographic accounts. In R. Fardon (Ed.), *Localising strategies: Regional traditions of ethnographic writing* (pp. 1-35). Edinburgh: Scottish Academic Press, and Washington, DC: Smithsonian Institution Press.

Fardon, R. (Ed). (1990b). *Localising strategies: Regional traditions of ethnographic writing.* Edinburgh: Scottish Academic Press, and Washington, DC: Smithsonian Institution Press.

Farran, D. (1985). Practices in the compilation of fieldwork notes. Occasional Paper No. 18, University of Manchester, Department of Sociology.

Galt, A. H. (1985). Does the Mediterraneanist dilemma have straw horns? *American Ethnologist, 12,* 369-371.

Geertz, C. (1960). *The religion of Java.* New York: Free Press.

Geertz, C. (1973). *The interpretation of cultures.* New York: Basic Books.

Geertz, C. (1983). Slide show: Evans-Pritchard's African transparencies. *Raritan, 3,* 62-80.

Geertz, C. (1988). *Works and lives: The anthropologist as author.* Cambridge, UK: Polity.

Gilsenan, M. (1990). Very like a camel: The appearance of an anthropologist's Middle East. In R. Fardon (Ed.), *Localising strategies: Regional traditions of ethnographic writing* (pp. 222-239). Edinburgh: Scottish Academic Press, and Washington, DC: Smithsonian Institution Press.

Goffman, E. (1961). *Asylums: Essays on the social situation of mental patients and other inmates.* New York: Doubleday.

Hammersley, M. (1991). *Reading ethnographic research: A critical guide.* London: Longmans.

Hammersley, M., & Atkinson, P. (1983). *Ethnography: Principles in practice.* London and New York: Tavistock.

Hannerz, V. (1969). *Soulside.* New York: Columbia University Press.

Harvey, L. (1987). *Myths of the Chicago school of sociology.* Aldershot, UK: Avebury.

Hawkes, T. (1977). *Structuralism and semiotics.* London: Methuen.

Herzfeld, M. (1984). The horns of the Mediterraneanist dilemma. *American Ethnologist, 11,* 439-454.

Herzfeld, M. (1987). *Anthropology through the looking-glass: Critical ethnography in the margins of Europe.* Cambridge, UK: Cambridge University Press.

Hippler, A. E. (1974). *Hunter's Point: A black ghetto.* New York: Basic Books.

Hobart, M. (1990). Who do you think you are? The authorized Balinese. In R. Fardon (Ed.), *Localising strategies: Regional traditions of ethnographic writing.* Edinburgh: Scottish Academic Press, and Washington, DC: Smithsonian Institution Press.

Hobbs, R. (1988). *Doing the business: Entrepreneurship, the working class, and detectives in the East End of London.* Oxford, UK: Oxford University Press.

Howell, J. T. (1973). *Hard living on Clay Street: Portraits of blue collar families.* New York: Anchor Books.

Jackson, J. E. (1990). Déjà Entendu: The liminal qualities of anthropological fieldnotes. *Journal of Contemporary Ethnography, 19,* 8-43.

James, W. (1990). Kings, commoners, and the ethnographic imagination in Sudan and Ethiopia. In R. Fardon (Ed.), *Localising strategies: Regional traditions of ethnographic writing* (pp. 96-136). Edinburgh: Scottish Academic Press, and Washington, DC: Smithsonian Institution Press.

Junker, B. (1960). *Field work.* Chicago: University of Chicago Press.

Kellner, H. (1989). *Language and historical representation: Getting the story crooked.* Madison: University of Wisconsin Press.

Krieger, S. (1979). Research and the construction of a text. In N. Denzin (Ed.), *Studies in Symbolic Interaction* (Vol. 2, pp. 167-187). Greenwich, CT: JAI Press.

Krieger, S. (1983). *The mirror dance: Identity in a women's community.* Philadelphia, PA: Temple University Press.

Krieger, S. (1984). Fiction and social science. In N. Denzin (Ed.), *Studies in Symbolic Interaction* (Vol. 5, pp. 269-286). Greenwich, CT: JAI Press.

Labov, W. (1969). *The logic of non-standard English.* Washington, DC: Center for Applied Linguistics.

Lacey, C. (1970). *Hightown grammar.* Manchester, UK: Manchester University Press.

Lederman, R. (1990). Pretexts for ethnography: On reading fieldnotes. In R. Sanjek (Ed.), *Fieldnotes: The makings of anthropology* (pp. 71-91). Ithaca, NY: Cornell University Press.

Lepenies, W. (1988). *Between literature and science: The rise of sociology.* Cambridge, UK: Cambridge University Press.

Lewis, O. (1961). *The children of Sanchez: Autobiography of a Mexican family.* New York: Random House.

Lewis, O. (1965). *La vida: A Puerto Rican family in the culture of poverty—San Juan and New York.* New York: Random House.

Liebow, E. (1967). *Tally's Corner, Washington, D.C.: A study of Negro streetcorner men.* London: Routledge and Kegan Paul.

Lofland, J., & Lofland, L. (1984). *Analyzing Social Settings.* (2nd ed.). Belmont, CA: Wadsworth.

Lutkehaus, N. (1990). Refractions of reality: On the use of other ethnographers' fieldnotes. In R. Sanjek (Ed.), *Fieldnotes: The makings of anthropology* (pp. 303-323). Ithaca, NY: Cornell University Press.

McCloskey, D. N. (1985). *The rhetoric of economics.* Madison: University of Wisconsin Press.

McDonald, M. (1989). *We are not French! Language, culture and identity in Brittany.* London and New York: Routledge.

56

McGrane, B. (1989). *Beyond anthropology: Society and the other.* New York: Columbia University Press.

Mishler, E. (1984). *The discourse of medicine.* Norwood, NJ: Ablex.

Moeran, B. (1985). *Okubo diary: Portrait of a Japanese valley.* Palo Alto, CA: Stanford University Press.

Moeran, B. (1990). Beating about the brush: An example of ethnographic writing from Japan. In R. Fardon (Ed.), *Localising strategies: Regional traditions in ethnographic writing* (pp. 339-357). Edinburgh: Scottish Academic Press, and Washington, DC: Smithsonian Institution Press.

Mulkay, M. J. (1985). *The word and the world: Explorations in the form of sociological analysis.* London: George Allen and Unwin.

Myers, G. (1990). *Writing biology: Texts in the social construction of scientific knowledge.* Madison: University of Wisconsin Press.

Nelson, J. S., Megill, A., & McCloskey, D. N. (Eds.). (1987). *The rhetoric of the human sciences.* Madison: University of Wisconsin Press.

Olesen, V., & Whittaker, E. (1968). *The silent dialogue: A study in the social psychology of professional socialization.* San Francisco: Jossey-Bass.

Parkin, D. (1990). Eastern Africa: The view from the office and the voice from the field. In R. Fardon (Ed.), *Localising strategies: Regional traditions in ethnographic writing* (pp. 182-203). Edinburgh: Scottish Academic Press, and Washington, DC: Smithsonian Institution Press.

Preston, D. R. (1982). Ritin fowlklower daun 'rong: Folklorists' failures in phonology. *Journal of American Folklore, 95,* 304-326.

Preston, D. R. (1985). The Li'l Abner syndrome: Written representations of speech. *American Speech, 60,* 328-336.

Rabinow, P. (1977). *Reflections on fieldwork in Morocco.* Berkeley: University of California Press.

Richardson, L. (1990a). Narrative and sociology. *Journal of Contemporary Ethnography, 19,* 116-135.

Richardson, L. (1990b). *Writing matters.* Newbury Park, CA: Sage.

Rose, D. (1989). *Patterns of American culture: Ethnography and estrangement.* Philadelphia: University of Pennsylvania Press.

Said, E. (1978). *Orientalism.* New York: Pantheon.

Sanjek, R. (Ed.), (1990). *Fieldnotes: The makings of anthropology.* Ithaca, NY: Cornell University Press.

Shotter, J., & Gergen, K. J. (Eds.). (1989). *Texts of identity.* London and Newbury Park, CA: Sage.

Simons, H. W. (Ed.). (1989). *Rhetoric in the human sciences.* London and Newbury Park, CA: Sage.

Spencer, J. (1989). Anthropology as a kind of writing. *Man, 24,* 45-64.

Spradley, J. P. (1979). *The ethnographic interview.* New York: Holt, Rinehart & Winston.

Strathern, M. (1990). Negative strategies in Melanesia. In R. Fardon (Ed.), *Localising strategies: Regional traditions in ethnographic writing* (pp. 204-216). Edinburgh: Scottish Academic Press, and Washington, DC: Smithsonian Institution Press.

Strauss, A. L. (1987). *Qualitative analysis for social scientists.* Cambridge, UK: Cambridge University Press.

Strauss, A. L., & Corbin, J. (1990). *Basics of qualitative research.* Newbury Park, CA: Sage.

Suttles, G. (1968). *The social order of the slum.* Chicago: University of Chicago press.

Tesch, R. (1990). *Qualitative research: Analysis types and software tools.* London: Falmer.

Todorov, T. (1984). *The conquest of America: The question of the other.* New York: Harper & Row.

Tonkin, E. (1990). West African ethnographic traditions. In R. Fardon (Ed.), *Localising strategies: Regional traditions of ethnographic writing* (pp. 137-151). Edinburgh: Scottish Academic Press, and Washington, DC: Smithsonian Institution Press.

Tyler, S. A. (1987). *The unspeakable: Discourse, dialogue, and rhetoric in the postmodern world.* Madison: University of Wisconsin Press.

Van Maanen, J. (1988). *Tales of the field: On writing ethnography.* Chicago: University of Chicago Press.

Werbner, R. (1990). South-Central Africa: The Manchester school and after. In R. Fardon (Ed.), *Localising strategies: Regional traditions of ethnographic writing* (pp. 152-181). Edinburgh: Scottish Academic Press, and Washington, DC: Smithsonian Institution Press.

White, H. (1973). *Metahistory: The historical imagination in nineteenth century Europe.* Baltimore, MD: Johns Hopkins University Press.

White, H. (1978). *Tropics of discourse: Essays in cultural criticism.* Baltimore, MD: Johns Hopkins University Press.

Whyte, W. F. (1981). *Street corner society: The social structure of an Italian slum.* (3rd ed.). Chicago: University of Chicago Press.

Williams, M. D. (1981). *On the street where I lived.* New York: Holt, Rinehart & Winston.

Wolcott, H. (1990). *Writing up qualitative research.* Newbury Park, CA: Sage.

Young, M., & Willmott, P. (1957). *Family and kinship in East London.* London: Routledge and Kegan Paul.

ABOUT THE AUTHOR

PAUL ATKINSON is Professor of Sociology and Head of the School of Social and Administrative Studies, University of Wales College of Cardiff. He took his B.A. in Social Anthropology at Cambridge, and his Ph.D. from Edinburgh. He has conducted and directed ethnographic research in a number of educational and medical settings. His publications include numerous articles and book chapters. He is author of *The Clinical Experience* (Gower, 1981), *Ethnography: Principles in Practice* (with Martyn Hammersley, Tavistock, 1983), *Language, Structure and Reproduction* (Methuen, 1985) and *The Ethnographic Imagination* (Routledge, 1990). A second edition of *Ethnography: Principles in Practice* is planned. Together with Sara Delamont and Odette Parry, he is currently researching the academic socialization of doctoral students in social science disciplines.